Understanding Attachment Injuries in Children and How to Help

A Guide for Parents and Caregivers

Also Available

M-MAT Multi-Modal Attachment Therapy:
An Integrated Whole-Brain Approach to Attachment Injuries
in Children and Families

by *Catherine A Young*

Visit the website: www.m-mat.org *for more information*

Training Opportunities

M-MAT Training Institute ~ MMATTI

www.mmatti.org

Understanding Attachment Injuries in Children and How to Help

A Guide for Parents and Caregivers

Attachment-Based Parenting
Addressing Developmental Trauma
for Adoptive, Biological, and Foster Parents
Guardians, Kinship and Other Caregivers

CATHERINE A. YOUNG

Granite Swan Press
Groveland, CA

For permission contact: permissions@graniteswanpress.com

ISBN 978-1-7335703-2-9
ISBN 978-1-7335703-3-6 (ebook)

Library of Congress Control Number: 2021930952

All examples and dialogue in this book are constructed from over 20 years of experience and do not represent any single individual or set of individuals. All names are entirely fictitious. Any similarity to real persons, living or dead, is coincidental and not intended by the author.

Excerpt from article, "Bonding and Attachment in Maltreated Children," by Bruce Perry, MD, Ph.D. (www.childtrauma.org).
Reprinted by permission.

Published by Granite Swan Press
P.O. Box 122
Groveland CA 95321
www.graniteswanpress.com

Visit:
Website: www.m-mat.org
M-MAT Training Institute: www.mmatti.org
Facebook: www.facebook.com/MultiModalAttachmentTherapy
YouTube Channel: M-MAT Training Institute ~ MMATTI
Instagram: www.instagram.com/multi_modal_attachment_therapy

It is to the brave parents, the exhausted parents, parents with hope and parents who are beginning to lose hope, whether biological, adoptive, foster, or kin, that I dedicate this book!

Contents

Acknowledgements   xi

Introduction   1

1 Orientation to this Book   5

   Purpose
   Terms
   Limitations of this Book
   Resources
   Hopes for this Book

2 Overview - Being an Agent of Change and Healing   9

3 Understanding Attachment and Your Child   13

   What is Attachment and Why is it Important?
   Understanding Children with Attachment Injuries
   Worldview of Children with Attachment Injuries
   Behavior Associated with Attachment Injuries
   Signs of Secure Attachment

4 Healing Concepts   31

   You are Important
   Relationship is the Key to Healing
   Parenting as Self Discipline
   Playing the Long Game
   It will Take Time
   Repetition is Your Friend
   Healing is a Process, Not a Destination
   Two Steps Forward, One Step Back
   Stay Calm

Stay Engaged
You Can't Control Your Child
Your Child Can Learn to Control Themselves
See Your Child's Best Self
Don't Take it Personally - Cover Your Buttons
Love is Not Just a Feeling
Perfection is NOT Expected or Required
Make Apologies
Guilt and Shame
Darkest Before the Dawn
Others May Not Understand
Self Appreciation

5 Creating Safety   **47**

Environment and Structure
Be A Safe Person
Provide Support
Make a Plan

6 Building Connection   **63**

Touch
Eye Contact
Singing and Rhythm
Mirroring
Fun and Play
Attachment-Based Play
Child-Led Play
Communication
Maintaining/Re-establishing Connection
Be Present
A Note for Foster Parents and Other Temporary Caregivers
Make a Plan

7 A New Story   **87**

Re-Storying
Positives in the Moment
A Time When...
Highlight Reel
Storytime
Talk About Your Child

Your Child's Story
Make a Plan

8 Attachment-Based Therapy   **99**

Why is Therapy Important?
The Failure of Traditional Therapies
Important Components of Attachment-Based Therapy
What to Avoid
Some Promising Therapies
Give it Time, but Not Too Much Time
How to Find a Therapist

9 Understanding Behavior   **111**

Attachment-Injured Children and Behavior
Understanding Emotional Dysregulation

10 Reducing Challenging Behavior   **115**

Structure and Environment
Behavioral Considerations
Communication
Teach Skills
Stay Out of Power Struggles
Take Care of Yourself
Make a Plan

11 Addressing Challenging Behavior   **147**

Remind
Repeat
Redo
Rethink
Restore
Givebacks
When Your Child is Emotionally Dysregulated
Create a Safety Plan
Tips for Addressing Behavior Successfully
Putting It All Together
Make a Plan

12 Getting Support   177

  Natural Supports
  Community Supports
  Schools
  Professional Supports
  Support Groups
  Respite
  Media
  Make a Plan

13 Self-Care   185

  Physical
  Mental
  Emotional
  Social
  Spiritual
  Make a Plan

14 Attachment & Mental Health Diagnoses and Terms   191

  Demystifying Mental Health Diagnoses
  Child Trauma and Attachment Terms

Final Thoughts   201

Appendix A: Attachment-Based Play Activities   203

Appendix B: Resources   213

  Attachment-Based Parenting
  Attachment-Based Therapy
  Communication
  Picture Books
  Well-Respected Authors in the Field

About the Author   217

Acknowledgements

I wish to thank the many parents and children with whom I have had the privilege to work. They have been as much my teachers as I theirs!

They say it takes a village to raise a child. Well, it certainly takes a village to write and publish a book! Those in my village who have provided invaluable support include Whitney, Teresa, Jennifer, Lisa, Amber and Ben. A heartfelt thanks!

Introduction

Children who have had difficulties or disruptions in their first, early relationship with their parent or primary caregiver often struggle with attachment injuries. These children frequently come to reject the very things they most need from their parents or caregivers: love, connection, and relationship. Their behavior can be challenging, perplexing, and/or hurtful. Parents and caregivers, and even many professionals, are often at a loss as to how to help.

If you are a parent or primary caregiver of an attachment-injured child, you are the person who is in the best position to help your child. But how do you help your child when they reject the very thing they need? When they actively turn away from the support you offer or seem indifferent to you as a caregiver? What do you do when the parenting strategies that have worked well for other children don't seem to work for this child?

I have worked for over 25 years with children and families struggling with attachment injuries. I have had parents come to me at their wits' end. Sometimes their child had been in therapy for years with no significant progress.

For many parents, it was hard to cope with the lack of connection with their child. It was hard to continue to try to parent a child who passively or actively rejected them over and over again. If you added to that extreme behaviors or behaviors that appeared to be intentionally hurtful, parents often felt ineffective, exhausted, and hopeless. Some wondered if someone else might be able to better help or parent their child.

For some parents, attachment theory was entirely new. No one had explained to them what attachment was and what happens when it is disrupted or injured, much less how to help. Others had gone to therapists who purported to be attachment therapists, but, upon examination of the therapy the child received, it was difficult to find the attachment-based interventions.

As a therapist seeking to help these children and families, I went in search of effective therapies. I discovered attachment theory and developed a new, integrated, attachment-based therapy model: Multi-Modal Attachment Therapy (M-MAT). I additionally applied what I learned to advise parents in attachment-based parenting ideas and strategies so they could further bring healing into their homes.

Using this approach, I saw significant, fundamental changes for children and families. Children who had not responded to other therapies were responding now.

I have watched deeply traumatized, angry, sad, hurt and hurtful children become happy, healthy, and emotionally connected.

My desire to promote healing for more children and families and share this model with other therapists led me to write my first book: *M-MAT Multi-Modal Attachment Therapy: An Integrated Whole-Brain Approach to Attachment Injuries in Children and Families*. That book outlines a new, structured therapy model for helping attachment-injured children and their families.

As parents continued to reach out to me, it became apparent that a book was needed for parents and caregivers. I wrote this book to help parents and caregivers understand the dynamics of injured attachment and, more importantly, how to help their child. *Understanding Attachment Injuries in Children and How to Help* provides the same theoretical background as the previous book, along with greatly expanded, practical, attachment-based parenting strategies.

Consider this book a conversation between you and me, reflecting the many conversations I have had with parents over the years. Look for the gems within that will help you on your own journey with your child.

1

Orientation to this Book

Purpose

The purpose of this book is to provide education and support to parents and caregivers to help them understand their child and be an instrument of change and healing in their child's life. It is a stand-alone book but is also meant as a supplement for parents who are engaging with a therapist in Multi-Modal Attachment Therapy (M-MAT) or a similar attachment-based therapy model.

While this book speaks specifically to parents of children with significant attachment difficulties, many of the ideas and strategies can be useful for all children and parents! Along the same lines, temporary caregivers and others in a child's life, such as childcare workers, teachers, coaches, and family members, will also find useful information herein.

Terms

Throughout this book, the terms "caregiver" and "parent" will be used interchangeably to mean a child's primary caregiver(s), whether that is a relative, foster or adoptive parent, biological parent, or guardian.

I will also use the term "attachment injury" rather than attachment disorder. Children with attachment injuries have a range of attachment difficulties, from mild to severe, with various presentations. I like the term attachment injury because it separates the child from the injury, and injuries can heal. Like the physical metaphor, some injuries require intervention to heal or heal well.

Additionally, the term reactive attachment disorder (RAD) has developed a lot of emotionally charged associations over the years and carries a stigma and negative expectations in the popular culture.

Finally, attachment disorders are narrowly defined professionally, and, often, children with attachment injuries are not diagnosed with an attachment disorder, as explained in chapter 14: Attachment and Mental Health Diagnoses and Terms.

I occasionally use the term "attachment-injured child" to indicate a child with moderate to severe, untreated attachment injuries. This is for ease of communication and not an attempt to label children. All children are more than their struggles, including children struggling with attachment injuries. Like any child, a child with attachment injuries may be bright, or musical, or creative, or have a good sense of humor, or display any other number of strengths that are a part of the whole person.

For ease of reading, "they" and its derivatives (their, them) will be used as needed for gender-neutral pronouns, rather than "he" or "she" or the more awkward "he or she" and derivatives. This is consistent with the way most people speak and evolving written norms.

Limitations of this Book

This book is geared towards children 5 to 12 years old. Much of it will also apply to younger or older children, yet teens and very young children may have developmental needs not specifically addressed in this book.

Just as it is difficult to cover all developmental ages in a book, it is impossible to cover all aspects of attachment injuries and parenting of attachment-injured children. When I work with families, I can provide support based on what I know about the family and their particular needs and belief systems. It is a give-and-take, two-way process. In a book, of course, I cannot do so. I have included what has seemed most helpful to the families with whom I have worked. I am hopeful it will be helpful to you and your family as well.

Resources

Attachment-based play activities are listed in Appendix A, and additional resources to explore are listed in Appendix B.

Hopes for this Book

My hope is that you, the parent or caregiver of an attachment-injured child, can find inspiration and help in these pages. I hope that no parent has to operate in the dark or sit helplessly by as their child just seems to get worse. I hope that you gain a better understanding of your child's inner world and needs, and your role and power in their life. I hope that you will find practical, useful strategies and tools within these pages. Ultimately, I hope for the healing of children and families.

2

Overview - Being an Agent of Change and Healing

No one is more important in your child's life than you. The relationship you develop with your child will have lifelong consequences for them in almost every area of their life. If your child struggles with significant attachment injuries, creating a healthy relationship will be a particularly challenging task. It takes more than good parenting skills. Your child has special needs that require a unique understanding of your child and specialized skills to help them overcome their relational hurdles.

This book will help guide you in being an agent of change for your child. Helping your child begins with understanding their inner experience and the dynamics that motivate and propel behavior. From this knowledge base, you can more intuitively respond to your child in helpful, healing ways.

Next are ideas to support a healing stance or attitude. This involves understanding your importance and role in your child's life and managing your own emotions, responses, and behavior. It in no way calls for perfection, only the willingness to develop discipline for yourself as a parent. This will be helpful not only for your child but for you as well in being a proactive, rather than reactive, participant in your own life and family.

Creating a physically and emotionally safe environment is the next necessary step in fostering growth and healing for your child. Safety is the container in which you will nurture your child's being.

Perhaps the most important of all the ingredients for healing is building the connection with your child. This is where the essence of healing occurs. By fostering connection with your child, you are directly addressing the injury that has impaired them, and exercising those parts of the brain that need development, i.e., the parts associated with relationship and attachment. Because your child is injured in the area of relationship, they require healing through relationship to make significant progress.

You can further advance this healing by helping your child create a new, positive, and healing story about their life, their family, and relationship. Because humans are cognitive beings, your child has created a cognitive structure or life story based on their early experiences. This life story is often maladaptive. Using strategies in this book, you can help them re-story their lives in an adaptive, helpful way.

Sometimes an outside third party is absolutely necessary for a child to even come to the table, as it were, to sample a new way of being and interacting. A therapist knowledgeable in attachment theory and interventions can help you and your child navigate the difficult territory between where you are now, and where you want to be. Chapter 8: Attachment-Based Therapy, discusses what to look for, and what to be aware of, when looking for a therapist for this work.

Children with attachment injuries often have difficult or challenging behaviors. Parents often find that normal parenting strategies do not work with their attachment-injured child. This is largely due to the impaired attachment and worldview that the child holds. Key to changing these behaviors is developing the connection, or secure attachment, with your child and helping them change their story. As their attachment becomes more secure, and their story shifts, parenting will become easier.

That being said, there are attachment-based strategies and basic parenting concepts that can help both reduce and address challenging behaviors in a way that supports the goal of healing for your child. These are included in chapters 10 and 11.

As a parent with an attachment-injured child, you will likely need to access support in the world around you, for both your child and yourself, to promote success. This may include friends and family, community organizations, schools, therapists, and other professionals.

It will also be important to take care of yourself. Taking care of yourself is critical in helping your child. You cannot nourish your child if your well is empty. Do you have strategies to ensure you are cared for as you care for your child? Self-care is explored further in chapter 13.

Finally, understanding terms and diagnoses associated with attachment injuries will help you access resources and interact with professionals and others around your child.

At the end of some chapters, there is a *Make a Plan* page where you can write down the ideas you would like to try. Alternately, consider starting a parenting journal or notebook where you can write down ideas, develop plans, and note progress. Perhaps start by attempting a few strategies that seem most important. Making a plan will make it easier to follow through.

This book offers discussion and ideas for all these aspects of being a healing agent for your child. Consider the ideas within, and use them to propel you forward on your own unique journey with your child!

3

Understanding Attachment and Your Child

Understanding attachment and attachment theory will allow you to understand how your child is injured and, therefore, how you can help them. It will help you have empathy for your child, understand the underpinnings of their behavior, and take their behavior less personally, enabling you to parent more confidently and better meet your child's needs. In short, better understanding your child will help you better parent your child.

What is Attachment and Why is it Important?

Attachment theory is based on the idea that the attachment, or connection, that a child forms with their primary caregiver during the first three years of life has a dramatic and profound effect on that child's development. Emotional, behavioral, moral, and relational aspects of the child's life are greatly impacted by their first relationships.

Attachment is defined by Bruce Perry, MD, Ph.D., as an enduring emotional relationship with a specific person that brings safety, comfort, soothing, and pleasure; and the loss or threatened loss of the person brings intense distress. Further, the child finds comfort and safety in the context of this relationship.

Note that the relationship is enduring and emotional and that it is with a specific person. For the infant to develop an appropriate attachment, there needs to be at least one specific, consistent person in their life that provides safety, soothing, comfort, and pleasure. The first, or primary, attachment, usually between infant and mother, sets the template for all future attachments or relationships.

When we consider how helpless an infant is, it becomes easy to understand the biological imperative for the infant to attach to a safe and stable adult. The baby simply cannot survive on its own. For the baby to survive, someone needs to be watching out for it. The baby needs to know who that person is, who they can rely on for safety, sustenance, and nurturing. Research is very clear that infants can very early distinguish their mothers from others. Through interactions with their primary caregiver, the infant's brain is stimulated and develops.

When experiences or conditions disrupt the normal development of healthy or secure attachment, the attachment is impaired, and we can say that the child has attachment injuries.

Bruce Perry, MD, Ph.D., succinctly ties attachment to early brain development in this passage from "Bonding and Attachment in Maltreated Children" (www.childtrauma.org):

The capacity and desire to form emotional relationships is related to the organization and functioning of specific parts of the human brain. Just as the brain allows us to see, smell, taste, think, talk and move, it is the organ that allows us to love -- or not. The systems in the human brain that allow us to form and maintain emotional relationships develop during infancy and the first years of life. Experiences during this early vulnerable period of life are critical to shaping the capacity to form intimate and emotionally healthy relationships. Empathy, caring, sharing, inhibition of aggression, capacity to love and a host of other characteristics of a healthy, happy and productive person are related to the core attachment capabilities which are formed in infancy and early childhood.

Thus, we can further view attachment injuries as the underdevelopment of portions of the brain. This is useful when we think of treatment, parenting, and care of the child and how to exercise those parts of the brain to increase the capacity for positive attachment.

It is important to note that your child's brain is still young and still has a great capacity to grow and change based on the input it receives. The term neuroplasticity refers to the ability of the brain to change and grow based on experiences. Neuroplasticity occurs throughout the lifespan, but never more so than in childhood. When we have experiences, those experiences cause neurons to fire, which affects the brain. Repeated experiences more strongly affect the brain, underlining the importance of repetition and consistency in healing.

Attachment refers not only to infant-parent relationships but to relationships with close friends, family, and partners as well. It is the first relationships, however, that set the stage for the child's subsequent relationships. The quality and nature of a person's later attachments, or their ability to attach at all, is strongly dependent on their first, primary attachment.

Attachment is not something the child does, or the parent does. Rather, it is the connection that is developed through the reciprocal interaction between parent and child. When the child cries, the parent responds. When the parent makes silly noises, the child smiles. Ideally, the parent is attuned to their child's signals, providing stimulation, comfort, and affection. Through positive interactions with their caregiver, the child forms a sense of self-worth, a sense of efficacy in the world, and a template for all future relationships.

A child's healthy attachment to their caregiver helps the child develop a positive sense of self, the ability to regulate emotion, a strong moral compass, resiliency in the face of challenges, prosocial behavior, and empathy towards others. Resiliency research indicates that even just one healthy attachment/relationship in a child's life has a strong impact on the child's resilience and well-being over time.

When a child's attachment has been significantly disrupted in the first few years of life, and has not been treated, the child may face issues of low self-esteem, difficulty regulating emotions, and lack of empathy towards others. They may display disruptive, anti-social, or even bizarre behaviors. Though these children may be bright, they will often struggle to cope with the challenges of life, and their ability to establish healthy relationships will be severely impaired. Anxiety, anger, and depression are common. Those trying to parent these children often feel like failures as nothing seems to work. Many adoptive and foster family placements fail due to unaddressed attachment injuries. Attachment injuries can equally be a concern for children in their biological homes when there has been early disrupted attachment.

A number of experiences or conditions can disrupt a child's attachment, thereby creating attachment injury. These include both caregiver factors and child factors. Caregiver factors include:

• Multiple, sequential caregivers - A child can benefit from multiple caregivers if these are co-occurring and consistent over time, as in an extended family. If multiple caregivers are sequential, however, such as a child moving from foster home to foster home, great damage can be done as the child never has the opportunity to develop a deep attachment to any single individual, and any attachment that has been formed is broken. By definition, foster and adopted children have suffered attachment injury, having lost at least one primary attachment. The more they move around from home to home, the greater the potential for injury.

- Impairment in the caregiver's ability to respond appropriately to the child - This may include anything from depression, illness, substance abuse, mental illness, domestic violence, prolonged separation, or a parent with their own attachment injuries impairing their ability to respond to their child.
- Abuse and neglect - Severe neglect can be even more damaging than abuse to a child's attachment. The child who is not responded to at all can be more injured in their attachment than the child who is responded to harshly. Perhaps one of the most difficult parenting patterns for a child to cope with is one of severe neglect with unpredictable, sporadic abuse.
- Custody issues may contribute to attachment difficulties - For instance, attachment injury can occur when the child moves from a more stable parent's home to a less stable parent's home. The child experiences abandonment by the relatively healthy parent to whatever dangers exist in the home of the unstable parent, thus impairing their attachment to both.

Child factors include:

- Anything that may impair a child's ability to respond to their caregiver, including the child's illness, chronic pain, disability, or extended separation from their caregiver.

Although different children will respond differently, generally speaking, the more severe, chronic, and pervasive the disruption, the higher the potential for harm. Not all children experiencing the above will have significant attachment injuries. There are protective factors such as other significant relationships, child temperament, and subsequent care, to name a few, that also play a role in health and injury.

In addition to individual costs of attachment injuries, there are also societal costs. Social service, health, and law enforcement costs can be related to attachment-injured individuals. If left untreated, attachment injury is passed from generation to generation along with cycles of abuse and neglect. For every child that heals from attachment injuries, there is benefit to the child, the family, and society at large.

For the purposes of this book, children with attachment difficulties will be defined as children with attachment injuries. The term attachment injury is more inclusive than attachment disorder and suggests a continuum of severity from mild to severe, and, like all injuries, there is an implied potential for healing.

Bear in mind that children with significant attachment injuries are often diagnosed with any of a number of mental health disorders, and are often not diagnosed with an attachment disorder. For more information on mental health diagnoses and terms that might be relevant to your child, see chapter 14.

Understanding Children with Attachment Injuries

When presenting on attachment, I only half-jokingly state that we all have attachment issues. Certainly, many people have early relational challenges with their parents. This is what can make even adult relationships so difficult. Most people, however, are able to work out their early relational issues throughout their lives and subsequent relationships, sometimes with the help of therapy. When the attachment injury is too severe, however, the child rejects exactly what it is they need for healing.

One way to conceptualize an attachment injury is as an anxiety disorder. The child becomes so anxious and phobic of relationships, while at the same time desperately needing healthy relationships, that they push away, in every way possible, from those who might help.

Think about a fear or phobia you or someone you know may have experienced. For myself, I get very nervous around heights. Once, when I saw someone I cared about standing closer to the edge of a cliff than I was comfortable with, I had to turn around and walk away. It was difficult to tolerate the fear or anxiety it created in me. If you know anyone with a true phobia, you will know that they will go to great lengths to avoid the thing they fear. The catch-22 for the attachment-injured child is that the thing feared is also the thing needed for healing. The attachment-injured child is generally not consciously aware of this internal dynamic, yet it underlies much of their behavior.

The first three years of a child's life are crucial in the development of appropriate attachments. Severe disruptions during this period can be very damaging. It can be difficult for caregivers to understand why their child is having such difficulties when they are now in a loving, supportive home. The problem is that the child holds in their body and mind the experience that relationships are hurtful, painful, and life-threatening and, additionally, that there is something wrong with them. Furthermore, from a neuroscience perspective, the parts of the brain involved in healthy attachment are likely underdeveloped, so the capacity for connection is impaired.

Take the example of a child that, for the first six months of life, lived with a parent that suffered from addiction and mental health disabilities. This parent was passed out when their child was crying for food or comfort. When awake, the parent was highly irritable and screamed at the baby when they fussed too much. The child was malnourished and underweight. Maybe the parent had a partner that was abusive to them.

Perhaps at six months, the baby is removed from the home due to severe neglect. The child is preverbal, but what they have already learned is that they have no power to control their environment (lack of responsiveness to their cries), and while there is a biological imperative for the infant to be close to the caregiver for survival, the infant has found that the caregiver has threatened their survival and is unsafe. It is unsafe to try and get needs met, but also unsafe not to. The infant has learned that the big people in their life are to be feared and avoided. The parts of the brain that would have been stimulated by healthy parent/child interactions have been understimulated. In the new home, the baby may be very quiet, avoidant, fussy, or alternately clingy and avoidant.

The new parents receiving this beautiful baby into their home may have no idea of the injury done to the child and the potential impact on the child's life, much less how to best support healing for the child. The child is already set up for lifelong difficulties. Fortunately, the child is young, their brain is still very young, and if the parents are knowledgeable and skilled in attachment-based parenting, there is a chance for healing.

Imagine, further, that this child stayed in their biological home until they were three years old. Maybe the parent was sometimes OK, but most of the time wasn't. The child now has an understanding of parent and relationship that includes unpredictable, dangerous, hurtful, and unhelpful. The child has learned that it is up to their 3-year-old self to get even the most basic needs met. The child cannot count on anyone.

Young children are naturally egocentric. That is, they feel that what happens in the world around them is directly related to themselves. They do not have perspective. So, tied to the idea that they cannot count on anyone is the belief that it is their fault. Something is fundamentally wrong with them for their parent to behave this way. The child is NOT OK, NOT lovable. There is no joy in this child's life.

The brain develops to 90% of its adult size by age three. In this case, this amazing brain development has largely centered on survival and creating this thought pattern or template in order to understand and cope in the world. Children with attachment injuries tend to have the following beliefs:

- Adults, and parents in particular, at best have nothing to offer and, at worst, are deeply hurtful.
- Relationships are unsafe, scary, and anxiety-provoking.
- They are unloveable/bad.
- There is no one they can depend on.

As a result, the child feels deeply alone, ungrounded, empty, and anxious, but does not know what they are missing.

Worldview of Children with Attachment Injuries

To understand the child's behavior and why traditional therapies have so often failed children with attachment injuries, it is useful to go further into the worldview of the attachment-injured child.

The attachment-injured child has organized their experiences into a story or narrative in which parents have little to offer, and may be very hurtful or scary. Even when circumstances have changed and/or they are placed in a new environment with loving, capable parents, the child sees only the facts and incidents that fit with the initial story or will bend and interpret facts to fit within that framework. The child holds a rigid and dysfunctional template for relationships.

In addition, when there has been severe neglect or an inconsistent, chaotic early environment, the child has not learned that what they do actually matters or makes a difference. The child has no sense of efficacy. The child does not develop a good understanding of cause and effect. Research confirms that children who experience early trauma have a deficit in their cause and effect reasoning.

Furthermore, the child feels deeply alone. There is no one the child can depend on. This creates a great deal of anxiety. To ward off this anxiety, the child often tries to control their environment and, even more strongly, tries to control interactions with their primary caregiver. The high anxiety associated with relationship, and the rigidity of the child's worldview, cause the child to push away from the things they need most for healing, closeness and attachment, keeping the attachment-injured child in a state of disconnect.

Behaviors Associated with Attachment Injuries

Although the child may not be consciously aware of them, their negative core beliefs about themselves, relationships, and caregivers are very rigid and do not change easily. They generate behavior that is self-defeating, destructive, perpetuates the faulty beliefs, and pushes away the very support they so desperately need. This behavior can include:

- **Easily emotionally dysregulated/difficulty calming** - Being emotionally dysregulated means being overwhelmed by, or having difficulty regulating, one's emotions. It occurs when a child is acting from the more primitive, emotional part of the brain. This can include unconsolable crying, or long temper tantrums and rages that can be highly disruptive to family functioning. Parents may report that they feel they need to walk on eggshells around their child.

  Difficulty in regulating emotions may stem from the lack of parental soothing and co-regulation when younger. Young children learn to regulate their emotions with support from their parents or primary caregivers. When they have not had that early parental support, they may not have the skills or brain development necessary for self-regulation. When you add trauma and loss, it is easy to see why these children may have difficulty managing their emotions.

- **Rejects adult efforts to help them calm** - This can be very frustrating to parents trying to help their child, particularly when their efforts seem to make things worse.
- **Will not seek out caregivers for comfort, sharing, or support** - Sometimes this child may appear pseudo mature, with a high level of independence and little need for their caregiver.
- **Poor eye contact or eye contact on their terms only** - One of a young child's primary ways of communicating and receiving information from their caregivers is through eye contact. In a healthy parent/infant interaction, the child will receive reassurance and validation from their parent through eye contact. Young children will also assess the safety of a situation with an eye contact check-in with their parent or caregiver. In an unhealthy situation, when all the child has received through eye contact is anger and hurt, or eye contact has been absent altogether, they will stop engaging in this way.
- **Primitive/injurious self-soothing behaviors** - This may include behaviors such as scratching themselves when in high distress or head banging. An older child may revert to thumb sucking, rocking, or other behaviors generally associated with younger children.
- **Controlling behaviors** - The child may seem to have a need to be in charge or in control of every situation, often challenging or arguing with adults. The child that has experienced parents who were either incapable of being in control, or, when in control, were scary and unsafe, has learned that to feel safe, they need to feel in control.
- **Fragile ego, poor winner/poor loser** - This child does not do well with competition. The core belief that they are not OK makes losing intolerable and winning something to

brag about in an attempt to keep at bay their bad feelings about themselves. They may also be hypersensitive to any kind of criticism or negative feedback from both peers and adults for the same reason.

- **Poor impulse control** - The child may have difficulty thinking before acting, leading to difficulties in school, at home, and with peers.
- **Hypervigilance** - The child is usually quite aware of what is happening around them, being extremely alert to any possible threat or danger. Their very survival may have depended on being able to read the cues in their environment and caregivers.
- **Aggression** - Kicking, hitting, scratching, and biting are not unusual. The child may also exhibit aggression towards pets and animals. Aggression may be due to emotional dysregulation, poor impulse control, the re-enactment of their own trauma, and/or expression of anger in unhealthy ways.
- **Splitting of adults** - The child may work at splitting the adults in their life as a matter of course. This may be going to different adults to get different answers or trying to get one adult to side with them against another adult (most often the primary caregiver).
- **Eating issues/food hoarding** - This may be related to early food deprivation and/or be symbolic of the nurturing they so desperately need. It is not unusual for parents or caregivers to find food stuffed in nooks and crannies in the child's bedroom or for children to sneak out at night to raid the refrigerator or cabinets.
- **Can be superficially charming** - This is a strategy that may have helped ensure the child's survival and allowed them to get at least some of their needs met. This can be particularly frustrating to parents when their child is charming with everyone else but angry, irritable, and dismissive with them.

- **Indiscriminate/poor boundaries with unfamiliar adults** - The child may go to anyone. They may jump in a stranger's lap. The child is seeking safety in an unsafe manner, and, for the unaware adult, this behavior may seem endearing. The connection, however, does not go very deep. In this child's world, one adult is easily exchanged for another adult. There is no discrimination, no particular connection to one adult. This behavior also sets the child up to be further victimized.
- **Lack of empathy** - The child's belief in a hostile world and that, at the core, they are not OK, along with their own deep neediness, makes it difficult for them to have empathy towards others.
- **Nonsense lying and storytelling** - Most children lie for a reason, either to get (e.g., a sweet) or to avoid (e.g., punishment) something. The attachment-injured child may lie for no apparent reason. Parents may report that the child will insist that the sky is yellow, or make up a story about something that happened at school that never actually happened with no apparent goal or reason. Sometimes they will tell very elaborate stories that are clearly not true. Sometimes these stories will have an ego protective or bolstering function, such as stories in which they beat up bad guys, or they have accomplished unrealistic things, or have possessions they do not have.
- **Bizarre behaviors** - These can include anything well outside the range of normal. An example might be a child who offers their urine to peers as "lemonade."
- **Peer problems** - Attachment-injured children will often have one of three ways of being with peers: They may be easily victimized and picked on due to their low self-esteem; they may be the bully or aggressor, again due to their low self-esteem (and it may seem a good alternative to being a victim, as no one wants to be a victim); or they may not seem to care about their peer interactions at all due to their disconnect with people in general. Sometimes a child

alternates between being a bully and a victim in their peer interactions. Sometimes children with attachment injuries will look to peers to meet their primary attachment needs. This is a strategy that is bound to fail as their peers are unable to provide them the nurturing, stability, limit setting, and maturity that they need. They may present as a leader or follower in these situations.

• **Anxiety and depression** - Attachment-injured children can also be highly anxious and often suffer from depression.

Of course, not all attachment-injured children will have all of these behaviors and each child is unique. Children with mild attachment injuries may function fairly well, perhaps struggling primarily with family or peer relationships. Children with more severe attachment injuries may have quite severe impairments. Below are a few examples of how more severe attachment injuries may manifest in children:

• 12-year-old is bright but is a bully and overeats. Child is big and hurts other children in sneaky ways, e.g., pushing and tripping, when no one is looking. Has no positive peer relationships. Appears to lack empathy. Attempts to control people and situations.

• 5-year-old has hour-long rages. Hits, kicks, throws things, screams. Scratches self, threatens to jump out of a window. Difficulty with both family and peer relations. Highly sensitive to perceived peer rejection.

• 11-year-old engages in nonsensical lying, baffling caregivers. Child has no peer connections, does not seem to want friends, and acts bizarrely with peers, e.g., offering dead bugs to eat as candy.

• 9-year-old attempts to push infant sibling out a second-story window. Avoids eye contact. Sneaks out of their bedroom at night. Hoards food.

• 4-year-old is bright and makes everything a battle. Argues about everything. Refuses cooperation with even simple tasks. Rages for extended periods. Is a master at engaging parents in nonsensical arguments.

- 13-year-old runs away from home often. "Hates" parent. Gets in trouble with peers. Is very promiscuous with unsafe sexual behaviors. Easily emotionally dysregulated wherein screams and yells and runs. Has tried various drugs. Is fully out of parental control. Sees any attempt of parent to help as an attempt to hurt.
- 8-year-old seems cute and charming outside the home but regularly assaults parent in the home, hitting, kicking, and scratching, leaving bruises and marks.

Young children with significantly injured attachment will often respond in one of two ways with others; either with inhibited attachment or disinhibited attachment.

With inhibited attachment, a child will act as if adults do not exist in their world. They have come to believe that adults have nothing to offer them. They do not come to adults for solace or safety or assistance. They do not look to adults for positive interactions of any kind. They have no positive expectations of adults. In their world, they have come to rely only on themselves.

By contrast, a child struggling with disinhibited attachment will go to anyone at any time. They do not differentiate between the familiar and the stranger. They do not develop specific attachments to anyone. People are interchangeable. Although they can be charming, their relationships are superficial. They have learned to look everywhere and anywhere to try to get their physical and emotional needs met.

This child may jump into the lap of a stranger or take the hand of someone they have never met, while at the same time being emotionally avoidant of their caregiver. If they start to get too close, they may then turn away from their caregiver and turn to someone less familiar to them to maintain a sense of emotional safety. They are vulnerable to being victimized due to their neediness and lack of discrimination and may be easily led into trouble by others.

Whether a child exhibits inhibited or disinhibited attachment patterns, their ability to form strong, positive, reciprocal (give and take) relationships is severely impaired. Those trying to engage in relationship with them will often feel manipulated because these children have not learned what it is to truly relate to another human being.   Sadly, while these children may feel empty inside, they do not really know what they are missing.

The attachment-injured child is likely to display their most challenging behaviors with their primary caregiver, usually the mother. All the rage, anger, and hurt is directed at the symbol of the person who was supposed to love them and be there for them unconditionally. Sometimes they appear to function well with others or in other settings so that people begin to question the mother or primary caregiver's competence. It is not at all unusual for the mother or primary caregiver to be blamed by others for the child's difficulties with the reasoning that the child, "Does not behave that way with me!"

Signs of Secure Attachment

A healthy attachment is called a secure attachment. The following are indicators of secure attachment:

- In a strange situation, the child will look back to their parent for reassurance/safety.
- The child tries to engage their parent for acknowledgment, e.g., "Look Mom! Look what I made!" or "Look what I can do!"
- The child comes to their parent for comfort when hurt or sad.
- The child comes to their parent for support in challenging or difficult situations.

- The child wants to do things for their parent, e.g., make a mother or father's day card.
- The child wants to, and enjoys, engaging with their parent, e.g., playing a board game together or doing jumping jacks together.

In therapy sessions, I know progress is being made when the child spontaneously wants to reciprocate with the adult, e.g., when we are sharing a snack at the end and the child wants to give the parent a snack.

4

Healing Concepts

This chapter touches on broad ideas and concepts that will set the stage for you to take a healing stance with your child.

You Are Important!

You are important! If you are the primary caregiver in the life of an attachment-injured child, you are the most important person in that child's life and the best chance they have for healing. Never mind that your child dismisses you and their teachers or other professionals may think you are doing something wrong. Never mind that your child seems to be angry at you all the time. Never mind that the parenting skills that have worked so well with other children don't seem effective with this child. Know that you are the most important person in your child's life.

It can be really easy to feel that you are expendable, that your child would be better off with someone else. It is easy to get discouraged when you don't see progress and your child stays disconnected or, even worse, seems to intentionally try to be hurtful to you. With appropriate attachment-based parenting and attachment-based therapy, there is hope for healing, and you are the most essential ingredient in that healing. You and your child no longer need to be the victims of the attachment injuries that have run your child's life.

Relationship is the Key to Healing

Because your child's injury is relational, the healing must be relational. Behaviors may need to be addressed, but you will be unlikely to be able to create sustained behavior change with your child until the relational wounds begin healing.

Parenting as Self Discipline

When I talk to parents of attachment-injured children, I tell them to think of parenting like they might some kind of zen discipline. You, as a parent, may need to train yourself and that training requires practice, a willingness to make mistakes, and a willingness to learn and grow. Like any mental or emotional practice, the first place to start is with yourself.

Playing the Long Game

Always try to keep in mind that you are in it for the long haul. Short term relief at the expense of long term goals will only cause disaster. For instance, if you have been doing well at not responding to your child's whining and argumentative tone, but give in one time to get some relief at the moment, you will find that you have made your job much harder in the long run because your child will have discovered that this behavior works, and so will become more persistent in the behavior.

Alternately, if you have been good about connecting with your child daily when you are out of town, and you gave them that expectation, but you let it slide because you are busy or tired, it may be much more difficult and take much more work to connect when you return.

Always try to keep in mind the impact of your choices as a parent on the long term goals of providing connection and healing for your child.

It Will Take Time

There is no magic bullet when it comes to healing attachment injuries. In fact, attachment injury is one of the most treatment-resistant psychological conditions in children. What is required are the right strategies with a large dose of persistence.

Give the ideas in this book time. Don't give up too soon. Look for the beginnings of connection with your child. With the interventions in this book and good, targeted therapy, I suggest that you wait twelve weeks to re-evaluate your approach. Look for the beginnings of change, a shift in the interactions with your child. Don't let a bad moment or bad day blind you to real progress.

I am not suggesting that a child's attachment injuries will resolve in twelve weeks, but that you will hopefully see some progress in the beginnings or furthering of attachment, enough to allow you to want to continue.

I find the thing that often wears parents out the most is the lack of connection from their child. Relationship requires reciprocity, give and take. Even infants provide this in interactions with their parents by smiling and cooing in response to a parent's engagement. It is naturally difficult to persist in any relationship without this feedback and reciprocity. Once you experience a positive shift towards connecting from your child, it will generally be much easier to continue.

Twelve weeks can seem like a long time or a short time depending on your perspective, but in the life of your child and family, it is not very long. Many parents come to me after spending several years in therapy with their child with no notable change. So, look for change, but be patient and persistent.

Repetition is Your Friend

Repetition is your friend. This goes hand in hand with persistence. Remember that you are trying to exercise those parts of your child's brain that were neglected earlier in their life. You are trying to strengthen the neural pathways for fun and connection and positive behavior. Repetition strengthens those pathways. So whether you are working with your child on safety, connection, re-storying or behavior, repetition is good. Just as repetition is important in building physical strength and skill, it is also important in building emotional strength and resilience.

Healing is a Process, Not a Destination

Healing is a process. For most of us, it is a lifelong process to become our best, whole selves. As we enter different developmental and life stages, we often re-process earlier experiences. The same will be true for your child. The goal during their early years is to help them develop a secure attachment, allowing them to access all the resources that relationship provides. This frees them to grow and move towards their best self.

Two Steps Forward, One Step Back

Behaviors will likely improve slowly over time. It is helpful to track the intensity and frequency of your child's behavior so that you can track their progress. Also, be prepared for your child to backslide in their behavior. It is often two steps forward and one step back.

If your child is finally making progress and then has a very bad day or a very bad week, it can be really discouraging. It can lead to feelings of hopelessness, as if things will never get better. For some parents, this is when they become the most discouraged. They had hope and now feel like nothing is working. Knowing that backsliding is normal and to be expected can help you be prepared.

It can also help to know that a backslide can actually be a sign of progress. Your child may be starting to connect or attach, making them uncomfortable, pushing them into fear, and thus they are reacting strongly to push away and disconnect. Side with your child against the impulse to push away. Address the behavior, but let them know you are still there.

Stay Calm

It is important to stay calm in the face of your child's behavior. Why? Well, simply put, to get upset, to become emotionally dysregulated (i.e., when emotions overwhelm thinking or reason) doesn't feel good, is helpful to neither yourself nor your child, may further damage the relationship, and will likely only feed the unwanted behavior.

OK, easier said than done, you say! Well, fair enough. I'm a parent too. I understand. Throughout this book, you will find ideas and strategies to help you stay calm in the face of attachment-injury driven behavior!

Stay Engaged

Attention is like gold in the realm of childhood. Your child needs your attention, and the only way they know how to get it may be through negative attention-seeking behavior. You may be thinking, I try to give my child positive attention, but they don't accept it! They reject it outright or act out when I say something positive to them. Thus, it is easier for us both if I don't say anything at all.

Keep in mind that behavior that is driven by attachment injury is designed to push you away, keep you at a distance, in order to maintain a sense of safety. But if you allow it to push you away, your child will not improve.

Maybe your child is able to play well for long periods by themselves, but when you try to engage, they become irritable and oppositional. It may be tempting to let sleeping dogs lie. While understandable, disengaging too much just feeds the attachment injury at the expense of your child and the relationship.

That is not to say that parents should not take breaks, have me-time and time away as needed, just that disengaging entirely is counterproductive. You do not want to allow the attachment-injury driven behavior pushing you away to be successful, or no healing will occur.

So the parent and child seem to be in a no-win situation, at the mercy of the child's attachment injuries. Don't worry; there is hope. Ways of engaging and building connection with your child will be discussed further in chapter 6: Building Connection. The important thing to remember here is that engagement with your child is important and necessary for healing attachment injuries.

You Can't Control Your Child

One of the things that often trips parents up is the desire to control their child in the moment. Short of physical restraint or intervention, you cannot control your child in the moment. Accepting this will provide you with a level of relief.

This does not mean that you are letting go of all control. You may not be able to control your child's actions, but you can control the environment of the home and your own responses, which will either increase or decrease behaviors. You can help your child gain control of themselves. You can control the structure you set up in your home, your expectations, how you communicate, and how you parent. You can also regain control of the home if your child's attachment-injured behavior has taken control of it. In any given moment, however, you cannot control your child. The ultimate goal is that your child will gain control of him or herself, with your support.

For example, your child may have taken something that belongs to a sibling and needs to give it back. They refuse to give it back and run behind the couch. It may be tempting to go behind the couch and physically take the item from them, but they could end up running further away, or trying to wrest it from them could generate further out of control behavior. They also do not learn anything from this approach.

Exactly how to deal with the above situation will be discussed in chapter 11: Addressing Behavior. But at the moment, letting go of the idea that you are going to control your child at that moment can allow you to relax a little bit, take a breath, and consider the best strategy or response that will meet your long term goals of helping your child control themselves and make good decisions.

Of course, safety issues may need to be addressed immediately with a physical intervention, but many behavioral challenges will not be safety issues.

Your Child Can Learn to Control Themselves

I have had parents say to me that maybe their child just can't control themselves. What I say to them is that if your child can't learn to control themselves, there is no work to be done. For your child to function in the world, your child needs to learn to control their behavior, and your child can learn to control their behavior.

We know that there are reasons for your child's behavior, not the least of which may be trauma and/or attachment injuries. Nevertheless, I have worked with children with very extreme behaviors and difficult histories, and they have all learned to control their behavior.

It takes all the things this book speaks of, i.e., connection, safety, consistency, time, and strategies for reducing and addressing behavior, for success, but it can be done. Your child's brain is still young. It can and will learn. Remember that experience changes the brain. Have faith in your child's ability to learn and grow into health.

See Your Child's Best Self

Always look for the good in your child. As challenging as your child's behavior might be, assume that somewhere inside is a beautiful being looking for love and connection. Assume, despite their behavior, that there is a child within that needs and wants your nurturing.

If the only time your child appears at peace is when they are sleeping, then take a moment to gaze upon your sleeping, peaceful child, and, if you can, imagine that peace in their daytime hours.

Don't Take It Personally - Cover Your Buttons

Don't take it personally. Don't let your child push your buttons. This is another one of those things that is easier said than done. Keep in mind that your child is reacting from primitive needs and fears. If your child is attachment-injured that means that they have an impairment in the area of relationship. Even if you do everything just right, they will have difficult moments. They may be angry and take it out on you. They may be experiencing something internally that you are not privy to. They may be tired. They may be triggered. They may just be trying to maintain emotional distance out of a need for safety.

Before I was a parent, I had worked with children for a number of years. I had the mistaken belief that, as a parent, if I behaved a certain way with my child, my child would necessarily behave in a prescribed way. What I discovered is that children come with their own stuff. They have their own personalities, their own tolerances, their own challenges. On top of that, their immature brains are just that, immature. They are not skilled at calming themselves or thinking through things. You can do everything correctly, and your child will still tantrum, have a melt down, or act out at times. For attachment-injured children, even if their behavior seems deliberate and personally directed at you, know that it is part of their injury.

Perhaps your child intentionally breaks something of yours. Perhaps your child tells a teacher that you have mistreated them when nothing is farther from the truth. These are symptoms of your child's injury. That does not mean that you should excuse or put up with this behavior - that would be as damaging as an overreaction - but knowing that it is not about you can help you moderate your response appropriately. Details of how to apply an attachment-focused approach to addressing behaviors are discussed in chapter 11.

If your child does push your buttons - and it has happened to all of us - becoming aware of your reaction and giving yourself time away to calm down and/or process is a great idea. It is always OK to tell your child, "We will discuss this later," as long as you actually come back later. Take the time to calm yourself and decide how you want to move forward with your child in a constructive manner.

Self-talk can be a useful tool in these situations. It is sometimes not the incident itself that is causing high distress, but the meaning we make of it. If an event particularly pushes your buttons, it might be useful to journal or talk through with someone the meaning you are making of that event versus what is really true. Often the meaning we make of events is somewhat removed from reality.

For instance, if your child yells they hate you and then acts out against you, this could trigger automatic thoughts or meanings of, "I'm not lovable" or "This child will never love me." Both are distortions. The child's reaction has nothing to do with your lovability, nor is it a predictor of their ability to love or develop a loving relationship with you. More likely, they are angry at the moment, possibly even reacting to something that has nothing to do with you, and are acting out the only way they know how. For children, the statement, "I hate you!" often simply means, "I'm mad!"

Later in the book you will find strategies for responding to these kinds of statements.

Love is Not Just a Feeling

Ok, so maybe you have moments, maybe lots of moments, when you are not feeling particularly warm and fuzzy towards your child, especially when they are acting out. That's OK. That's normal. Love is not just a feeling. Wanting the best for your child, striving to be a better parent, feeding, clothing, and engaging your child, and protecting your child, are all love.

Maybe you have feelings of anger or sadness or hurt related to your child. Give yourself permission to have your feelings and still love and care for your child. Process those feelings however you need to, i.e., talk to friends, journal, seek therapy, etc., but be kind to yourself. Be kind to your child.

Perfection is NOT Expected or Required

No parent is perfect. We could all do better. It's OK. Your child isn't as fragile as you may think. Your child has survived difficult circumstances and is a warrior in their own story. They may be confused about who the enemy is, and their strategies may be limited and counterproductive, but your child is a survivor and a fighter.

Reasonable parenting strategies will not harm your child. Occasional parenting errors will not harm your child. You can relax. While you may feel ineffective, you will not damage your child with normal healthy parenting strategies, nor occasional errors, like yelling at your child or saying something you don't mean. These things can be corrected, and may even further the relationship if corrected.

You also are not expected to be 100% there for your child because it is not possible. Sometimes you will be distracted, sometimes you will not be at your best, and sometimes you will be busy with something else. That's OK. That is true of everyone. Just do your best. Part of your child's journey will be learning to respect that other people have needs, that people are human, people are not perfect, and that is OK.

Your child is injured, and the nature of their injury is that, without intervention, it is unlikely to get better and may get worse over time. You are not a failure. Your child needs specialized parenting and therapy strategies. In this book, we want to move from doing-no-harm to a place of healing for children with attachment injuries.

Make Apologies

Part of being strong is acknowledging mistakes without giving up your power or abdicating your parenting role. It is OK to say to your child, "I am sorry I yelled at you. I am working on doing better," while still addressing your child's behaviors. Each of you is responsible for your own behavior. This models for your child how to take responsibility appropriately.

Guilt and Shame

Guilt and shame can be factors in parenting. First, let's differentiate between guilt and shame. Guilt is the idea that I have done something wrong, and I feel bad about it. I would like to do better. Shame is the idea that I have done something wrong, and therefore I am bad (or a bad parent).

Shame is destructive to positive parenting. We are all people; we will all make mistakes. Your child does not need a perfect parent (as mythical as a unicorn). Your child needs you, warts and all. Many people, and perhaps parents in particular, have been conditioned to have shame responses. If you can become aware of your shame responses, you can try self-talk, "Yes, I yelled at my child. I wish I had not yelled at my child. I will work to do better in the future." That work may include learning or practicing some self-calming strategies, using more positive self-talk, and/or therapy for yourself to overcome triggers or shame responses.

Guilt is a more adaptive response. It is part of our internal navigation system that allows us to self-correct. As human beings, we are not perfect, and it is a natural human inclination to strive to do better. If guilt motivates us to make efforts to do better, then it serves a positive purpose. Always, though, exercise compassion and understanding for yourself. It will help you be a better parent and help you exercise compassion and understanding for your child.

If guilt feels overwhelming, it is probably shame that you are experiencing. Again, working with a therapist, journaling, and self-talk can help.

Guilt or shame can lead to shame or guilt-based parenting. In guilt-based parenting, the parent tries to make up for their failings with their child, or the child's early deprivation and abuse by another, by giving in to their child or over-indulging their child. This is a complete disaster for the attachment-injured child. All children need appropriate limits and boundaries, but none more than the child struggling with attachment injuries.

In shame-based parenting, the parent feels that they are a bad parent, feeling completely incapable and often just giving up. If you believe you are a bad parent, it is very difficult to do the work necessary to help yourself and your child, and it is the first thing that needs to be addressed.

If you are your child's biological parent, or in some way contributed to your child's early experiences that led to attachment difficulties, the pull to guilt or shame-based parenting may be particularly strong. Your child may even try to use your guilt or shame to manipulate you.

What your child needs is to know that you are strong and that you will set limits and boundaries to keep them safe. As a parent, let go of any shame, it is only toxic, and use any guilt you may have to help you be the parent your child needs. You can't change the past, but you can act in the present and create a better future. Get support, if you need it, from therapy and/or parenting and support groups.

Darkest Before the Dawn

I have discovered an interesting phenomenon in working with children and families. When I have been working with parents and children for several weeks, sometimes the parent comes to me and says they are not sure they can do it anymore; they are truly at their wits' end. I have found that if the parent can stick with it, the child usually makes a shift within a week or two. There is some kind of breakthrough in connecting.

It is almost as if the attachment injury is making one last push to distance, and the child feels the ambivalence of their parent. If the parent hangs in there just a little longer, there seems to be a letting go or giving in that happens on the part of the child that allows for the beginning or furthering of attachment.

This, of course, is anecdotal and just my interpretation of this phenomenon, but the point is to know that it can be darkest right before the dawn. The child may be beginning to feel connected, leading to a reaction to pull away as hard as possible. This can be a strong sign of progress. If the parent can persist, this can result in a breakthrough.

Others May Not Understand

Be prepared for the possibility, even likelihood, that others won't understand. Teachers or other family members may not understand your child's dynamics. They may believe that your child's behavior is due to something you are doing wrong. Family members may undermine your parenting while trying to be helpful, or because they feel sorry for your child.

You may need to provide education to others in your child's life, particularly if they have a significant role, about your child's difficulties and your approach. You may want to give them this book if you think it will be helpful. Helping others understand may be a part of being a good advocate for your child.

Some people on the periphery, such as peers' parents, you may just need to not worry about. Some people may not understand, some people may never understand, and that is OK. If they are not directly involved in your child's life, they don't need to understand. You can still parent your child in a healing, attachment-based way.

Self Appreciation

Give yourself a pat on the back. If you are even reading this book, you are trying to make a difference in your child's life. Good for you! Find ways to appreciate yourself! Have a special dinner, take a bath, say something nice to yourself, talk to or spend time with someone who appreciates you. Right now, and at any moment, you can appreciate yourself for caring and doing your best!

5

Creating Safety

Safety is the first necessary condition for your child's healing. It is the environment in which you and your child will grow and nurture the connection that will lead to emotional health. Your child will not likely get better if they do not have safety. They are already acting from an anxiety/fear attachment-injured place. When your child is in anxiety or fear, they cannot easily access the prefrontal cortex, the reasoning part of their brain. They will have difficulty processing information and making good decisions and will be unable to relax into any kind of attachment.

Safety is a necessary, but not entirely sufficient, condition for healing attachment injuries. The attachment-injured child has an anxiety response to relationship itself and a rigid view of the world. It will take a concerted effort on the parent's part to help their child overcome these, but no progress can be made without safety. So, safety first!

Children with attachment injuries have often had multiple unsafe or scary experiences, making them even more susceptible to fear reactions. Your child may quickly go into a fear/panic response, activating the part of their brain that governs the fight, flight, or freeze response. As a result, they may quickly become emotionally dysregulated and engage in impulsive, aggressive, or unsafe behavior, or they may withdraw completely. While they are in fear, they will not be engaging those parts of the brain that support relationship and connection, and their body will be flooded with stress hormones.

It is helpful to recognize that even if a person is safe, they might not feel safe. So, even if your home is very safe, your child still may not feel safe.

I will give an example from my own life. I was once attacked by four dogs at once. It was a very scary experience for me. Some time afterward, I was at a meeting. Someone came in with their dog, who was on a leash and quite well behaved. They sat some distance behind me. At the sound of the dog's collar jingling, my adrenaline shot up, and I did not feel safe. I was able to logically see that I was perfectly safe. It was a nice dog, well behaved, and under the control of its owner. It did not matter. The stress hormones had already activated.

It is interesting to note that not only did I find myself triggered by the sound of a dog collar jingling, I also went into alert when I heard keys jingling. Keys may seem fairly removed from a dog attack. Still, the sound was similar enough to the sound of dog collars jingling, which had been recorded in my brain with a danger alert, that my body reacted. In the same way, your child may be triggered by sights, sounds, smells, tastes, and touch that may be only distantly connected to the trauma they experienced. Note that these reactions are automatic, occurring before there is a chance to think about or process what is happening.

Think further about a phobia you, or someone you know, may have, maybe spiders or heights or closed places. In the face of those triggers, even if a person knows they are perfectly safe, they do not feel safe.

One well-researched way that phobias are treated is through something called exposure. Exposure is exposing your child to the home and yourself, and the relationship, which is obviously going to happen naturally, while consistently being a safe home and safe person. By providing a safe home and being a safe person, you will set the stage for building connection, further increasing your child's sense of safety and, ultimately, healing.

Over time I became less reactive to dogs. This was because I was not re-traumatized, and I was exposed to numerous situations with safe dogs. Children with attachment injuries have often experienced multiple traumas, so the fear response is more deeply ingrained and more difficult to soothe.

The baseline requirement for healing is safety. Safety is the container in which you will plant and grow the seeds of relationship with your child. As the adult in the relationship, you are the one responsible for setting and maintaining safety. I've organized ways of creating safety into 3 different categories: environment and structure, being a safe person, and providing support. Consider the following ways of creating safety.

Environment and Structure

Your home's environment and the structure you create throughout the day can support your child's feelings of safety and security.

Routine and Predictability

Routines create predictability and, therefore, a sense of safety. Consider developing some kind of daily routine to help your child manage through the day. Having a morning routine and an evening routine can be particularly helpful, and eating meals together at a predictable time helps build family time into your day. Consistent structure will help your child; inconsistent structure may make things worse.

Perhaps wake your child up in the same way every morning, maybe with a gentle rub on the back or a morning song. At night, toothbrushing, bath, and reading to your child can all make for a soothing and predictable routine.

For children who have difficulty remembering a routine or who seem anxious about it, try posting a daily, morning, or evening schedule somewhere your child can easily see, perhaps with bright colors and pictures.

Other ways of creating predictability include talking to your child every night about what the plan is for the next day, or talking to your child as you take them to school about what the plan is for after school. The more your child can anticipate what is going to happen, the less anxious they will be.

If there is a sudden change in plans, let your child know as soon as practically possible. Ask if your child has questions about any different or new events. Provide as much information as you can.

Maintain Calm

Try to maintain a reasonably calm environment. I once observed an 8-year-old child in a group home setting. We were outdoors where there was a lot of chaos, with children running and yelling and no calm space. The child I was observing, who had PTSD (posttraumatic stress disorder), was unable to relax at all. This child stayed in a heightened state of alert, or hypervigilance. No one was being hurtful, but the environment itself felt unsafe to the child.

Your child may or may not respond well to playful chaos. If you have a large family, some chaos is inevitable. Observe your child for signs of stress during more chaotic moments and during the aftermath. Some children may be OK at the moment but have a meltdown afterward. Consider creating a calm cubby for your child as described below so that your child can remove themselves from the chaos.

Of course, maintaining a calm home means that the adults need to remain calm. Fighting and arguing among adults causes a great deal of stress for children. Naturally, there are going to be disagreements between adults living together. Make a plan with the adults in the home that any disagreements be discussed away from your child(ren). This will help all the children in the home. Come up with this plan ahead of time. That way, if an argument begins, one of the participants can say, "We should discuss this later," or something similar, with the agreement to do so.

It is especially important not to argue about your child in front of them. Every child who witnesses the adults around them argue about them, or their care, feels that it is their fault. This is a big burden for a child to carry and only confirms the child's faulty belief that they are bad, or something is wrong with them.

Plan time away from your child to talk about your child's care. Present a unified front to your child. This will help them feel safe and secure in the family and may derail their efforts to split or manipulate the adults.

Create a Calm Cubby

It can be useful to have a quiet or calm, comforting space within the home that your child can retreat to if they need or want to. This could be a bedroom, a cozy corner, or a child's tent somewhere in the house with blankets, stuffed animals, and quiet toys. Your child can help decide what they would like to have in their quiet cubby.

Alternately, there may be an outside space that can function in this way, such as a playhouse, small garden, tent, or fort. The idea is that there is someplace your child can go to experience calm, quiet safety.

Monitor for Safety

Any child who has experienced early trauma is likely to be very sensitive to the possibility of threat. Monitor for conditions that may lead to your child feeling unsafe, either physically or emotionally. This may include apparently innocuous factors such as voice tone or facial expression of the parent, or more obvious factors such as yelling, chaotic or unexpected changes, or exposure to television or media violence or sexual content. Your child may have some triggers that are very specific to them. Due to their attachment injury, your child will likely not seek you out for safety or comfort, so it is up to you to approach them and check in or offer support.

Maintain a Non-Violent Home

This is probably obvious, but parents need to be non-violent in their approach. This includes:

- No corporal punishment. This includes spanking, washing a child's mouth out with soap, putting hot sauce on a child's tongue, making a child take a very cold shower, or anything that creates a high level of physical discomfort. Corporal punishment will only make your child worse. It will confirm the idea that they are bad and you are bad; create continued anxiety; and make both you and your home feel unsafe.

  Your child may already associate pain with relationship or closeness or love. This is an association you do not want to reinforce as it will set them up for problematic relationships throughout life.

  Also, the research is clear: Children who experience corporal punishment have more behavior problems and are more aggressive than those who don't.

- No violence between the adults in the home. Adults need to model calm problem solving, and heated issues between adults should be discussed away from children. If there is domestic violence in the home, get help. Find resources in your community to help you deal with this and find safety for you and your child.

- Address sibling violence. When parents and adults are aware of violence between children and don't address it, it is seen as implicit condoning of the violence. The strategies for addressing behavior in chapter 11, including give-backs, can be used to address sibling aggression. It can also help to have house rules that include some version of *we respect other people's bodies* or *gentle touch only*. See more about house rules in chapter 10: Reducing Behavior.

Eliminate Exposure to Media Violence

It isn't unusual for children with attachment injuries to be drawn to violent content in television, movies, and video games. Unfortunately, exposure to media violence just reinforces the trauma and violence they may have experienced. Visual media bypasses the frontal cortex and goes straight to the visual cortex, which is tied to the emotional centers of the brain. A child experiencing violence on a monitor has similar brain and body reactions as a child actually experiencing violence. No child can heal with this repeated assault on their system.

Violence in media may also reinforce the idea of violence as a solution or way to manage in the world. If your child experienced violence at a young age, there is already a pattern or template in their brain for acting out violently. You do not want your child to exercise that pattern and cause it to become more ingrained.

Your child needs you to be their protector in this. They may not like it, and may actively oppose restrictions, but, somewhere deep down, they probably know that this exposure to violence is not good for them, and they may even experience a sense of relief.

Create Food Security

Many children with attachment injuries have had the experience of food deprivation. If this was the case with your child, they need to know that food is available. You may want to keep a bowl of fruit or other healthy snacks on the counter with the rule that it is always an option. It may also help your child to have a general meal and snack schedule, so they know when they can expect a full meal or snack. You can additionally verbally reassure them that you will always make sure they have food to eat.

Some children can be very picky eaters. There may be any number of reasons for this, including sensory issues, taste preferences, trying to control their environment, or more. Regardless of the reason, if this is the case for your child, an easy strategy is to have available a food option for meals that they can choose and generally will eat. Do not make it their favorite food. Make the alternative something that they can easily make themselves, such as a sandwich, which is always an option if they refuse the meal. This keeps you out of power struggles around food and provides a sense of food security for your child.

Never use the loss of food as a consequence for your child. The old fashioned, 'going to bed without your supper,' is not a good plan.

Just being aware of your child's anxiety around food can help you be sensitive to this need.

Be a Safe Person

If your child is attachment-injured, and you are their primary caregiver, they will automatically view you as an unsafe person due simply to your role in their life. This is not necessarily a conscious view, but it informs their behavior. While that will take time to change, you want to be safe for them.

Say What You Mean, Mean What You Say

First, say what you mean, mean what you say, and always follow through. Attachment-injured children generally have the experience that parents or caregivers are extraordinarily inconsistent. Give them a different experience.

Don't make empty promises. If you say you are going to be there, show up. If you say you are going to do something, be sure to do it. Of course, sometimes life intervenes, and we cannot always do what we plan. If this occurs, be sure to let your child know both that you wanted to follow through and what happened to prevent it. If there is a way to make up or reschedule, do that.

Likewise, consistency in discipline is important. Again, say what you mean and mean what you say. Don't make hollow threats. Sometimes parents of attachment-injured children get so frustrated with their child that they set consequences that they regret (e.g., you are grounded for a month!). In these instances, you can allow your child to earn their way back into good graces. This can be through doing chores, demonstrating cooperation in some specific way, etc. Whatever you choose, it needs to be clearly stated to your child, so there are no surprises.

The more consistent you can be in your word, whether with discipline or promises, the safer you will be for your child. When your child fully experiences that you mean what you say, they will be able to start developing a sense of trust and safety.

Voice Tone

Your child will respond to your tone of voice before your words. Your child may even be hypersensitive to your voice tone, thinking you are yelling at them when you are just being stern.

Most children will respond best and feel safest with a positive, upbeat tone, reserving a lower, firm yet calm tone for serious situations.

Each child is different. Some children may respond well to a stern tone when needed for setting limits, while other children may respond much better with a softer tone. I knew one child who, if their parent moved into even a slightly irritated tone, would dig their heels in, becoming completely uncooperative and uncommunicative. They responded much better when an upbeat tone was used throughout, even if it was the fifth time the parent was making a request.

When giving directions, use a positive or matter-of-fact tone that implies that you expect the direction to be followed. Avoid using a questioning or uncertain tone of voice when you need something from your child. This will only invite non-compliance.

Become aware of your voice tone. Be firm when you need to, but, when you can, try lifting your voice to a more positive note.

Stay Calm

Being a safe person also includes keeping yourself calm, which may involve learning some self-calming strategies, such as deep breathing or mindfulness exercises, and/or learning to take space when needed. Avail yourself of resources (e.g., books, online information, consult with others, etc.) as needed, to find what the best self-calming strategies are for you. If you just need to take space, let your child know and assure them that you will come back. This reduces anxieties around abandonment. An example, "I need some time to think. I'll check back with you in a few minutes."

Be In Charge

Your child needs you to be in charge. As much as they may fight against it, ultimately, they need to know that you are in charge so they can relax and be a child.

An overly permissive approach will create anxiety and lead children with attachment injuries to feel unsafe. They will often jump into a controlling mode if they sense hesitancy or uncertainty from you. Your child will feel safest when they know that a safe adult is in charge. It may take a while for your child to understand that you are safe and to let go of control, but that is the work. They will not benefit by being left to their own devices or being given too much leeway. In fact, children with attachment injuries need more structure and guidance than securely attached children to feel safe.

Reassure Your Child: You've Got This!

Children with attachment injuries are often anxious about things that they are not responsible for, like what's for dinner, or getting someplace on time, or getting the car fixed. You may see this in multiple or repetitive questions. While this may be annoying, it can help to understand that this may be coming from their experience of a place or time when they did have to take on adult responsibilities, and/or the adults in their life were not handling things.

Whatever your child's worry, let them know you've got it; they don't have to worry about it. You will make sure...(there is enough food, you'll get there on time, that the car gets fixed). Letting them know there is an adult in charge who can handle things helps create safety. You can do that through a simple statement, i.e., "It's OK, you don't need to worry about it. I'll make sure....I've got this! (playfully)."

Let Your Child Know You are There

You help soothe abandonment fears by letting your child know that you are there for them. If you are the forever home or parent for your child, you might jokingly tell them they are stuck with you. You were there yesterday, you are there today, you will be there tomorrow. There are some great picture books that relay this message (see Appendix B: Resources). Using picture books is further discussed in chapter 7: A New Story.

When there is a break for any reason, always let your child know when you will be back and/or when you will talk to them again. In the morning, when you drop them off for school, make it a habit to say, "see you after school!" or for other activities, "See you after practice (when I get back from the store, at 4:00, etc.)." It may even be useful when tucking them in at night to say, "See you in the morning."

Never leave your child without them knowing you are leaving. It may be very tempting to sneak off to the store while your child is playing, and your parenting partner can watch them, especially if goodbyes always seem to involve a lot of drama, but don't. Instead, tell your child where you are going and when you'll be back, and who is in charge when you are gone. This will create predictability, reduce anxiety around abandonment, and let them know someone is always watching out for them.

If you will be gone for an extended period of time, make sure you schedule phone calls or regular contact, and your child knows when that will be.

Relationship Development

It is good to note that one of the most significant ways of creating safety is helping your child develop a secure attachment. We all feel safer in the world when we have positive, secure attachments to others. Creating a safe environment creates space for that attachment, and developing a stronger attachment creates further safety. Building connection with your child is discussed in detail in the next chapter.

Provide Support

Your child will likely need extra support from you in anxiety provoking situations.

Help Your Child Manage Chaotic Situations

Life, of course, can't always be calm. Watch your child and see how they respond in more chaotic situations. Provide a quiet, safe place if you can, or the ability to opt out of highly chaotic situations if that is possible.

Some children may be drawn to chaotic situations, as it may more closely represent what they know. This does not mean that it is good for them. Use your parental discretion. See how they respond in those settings. See if they can maintain appropriate behavior. Do they appear comfortable or anxious? Observe how they respond after the event or leaving the setting. Do they have a meltdown? Do they have difficulty unwinding, coming back to baseline calm?

If you need to be in a less structured setting, perhaps another child's birthday party, and you know it will be difficult for your child, try some modifications. First, be sure to let your child know what to expect in the situation, including your expectations for their behavior and options if they are having difficulty. Let them know that you are trying to help them to have fun and be successful.

For example, it may help to keep your child near you in chaotic environments. Holding their hand or putting an arm around their shoulder may be useful. It is OK to tell them that they need to sit next to you or hold your hand, if that is what they need. If they are not near you, check in with them throughout. Finding a way for your child to take space from the group may also be useful. Limiting the amount of time, either coming late or leaving early, may be a good strategy. Assisting your child to manage in these settings helps create safety for your child.

If your house naturally has a lot of commotion, or even if it doesn't, you may want to try creating a calm cubby as described previously in this chapter.

Check in, Describe, Reassure, Plan

If there has been a chaotic event or you suspect your child may be triggered, check in with them. Provide comfort and reassurance when needed. Note that children with attachment injuries may reject a parent's attempts to comfort, but make the attempt anyway, letting them know you are there for them while being respectful of their boundaries.

For unexpected disruptive events, give an age-appropriate description of what has occurred and how it was handled. Ask your child what they noticed, including what they saw or heard, and how they felt or are feeling. For instance, say there was a fire in the kitchen, and you were able to put it out. You could say something like:

> The oil in the frypan caught on fire! The fire alarm went off. That was loud! I put it out by putting the lid on the pan and turned off the fire alarm. Everyone is safe, and everyone is fine. I will always make sure that everyone is safe in this house. What did you notice?... What did you hear or see?... How are you feeling?

If appropriate, do some safety planning. Your child will feel more comfortable and less vulnerable knowing there is a plan:

Do you remember what to do when there is a fire in the house?

This can also be done with the whole family after a difficult or traumatic event, allowing all parties to share their experience and plan together.

Discuss What To Do if Your Child Feels Unsafe

Discuss with your child what they should do if they ever feel unsafe. Included in this should be going to you and other supportive adults. Your child may not know how to do this as it may not have been an option in their early experience. They may not know what a safe person is. You may want to brainstorm a list of adults they can go to and role-play going to an appropriate adult. Try role-playing different settings, i.e., going to an adult at school, home, daycare, or a friend's house.

Be sure your child understands the difference between a stranger and someone familiar, such as a teacher, parent, known friend, or family member. You can brainstorm with them, at an age-appropriate level, how they know a person is safe. This may include things like:

A safe person is someone who:
They and their parents know
Talks respectfully to them
Does not hurt them
Does not ask them to keep secrets

Learning that adults can be sources of safety changes the story from "I'm on my own, no one can help me" to "I can get help, I have grown-ups in my life who will help and protect me." It is also empowering for your child to have some concrete strategies that move them from the powerless infant place to a place of power.

Make a Plan

There are probably many things you do to create safety for your child. Are there additional things you would like to try? Be as concrete and specific as you can:

1._____

_____

2._____

_____

3._____

_____

4._____

_____

5._____

_____

6

Building Connection

The emotional connection or attachment between you and your child is the foundation upon which your child will build the structures of their life. If the foundation isn't sound, the rest will feel precarious and unstable. Your child was injured in relationship, and so needs to be healed in relationship.

Once your child begins to connect or attach in a healthy, secure way, everything else, including addressing behavior, will be easier. Of course, the challenge with the attachment-injured child is that they push away the connection they need.

Touch, eye contact, singing/rhythm, mirroring, and play are all ways parents naturally connect with young children and are the keys to building connection with your child. These all come together in attachment-based play. Attachment-based play is the work-engine of developing attachment with your child.

Child-led play and communication skills can also support connection, along with strategies for maintaining and re-establishing connection.

Touch

If there were only one action, one thing I could recommend to strengthen your child's connection to you, it would be to increase positive physical touch with your child.

Touch is crucial not only to the development of attachment but also to overall child development and even survival. Failure to thrive has been linked in some cases to lack of touch, as have poor physical and mental development.

One of the first ways an infant interacts with their caregiver is through touch. Parents use touch to soothe, comfort, cuddle, and communicate with their babies. Touch is, by definition, connecting. The physical connection through touch is a good metaphor for the emotional connection children need. Attachment-injured children often have not received adequate touch and/or have received hurtful touch. It is not unusual for them to avoid touch or to only use touch in aggressive or controlling ways.

Some people may question the use of touch with children who have experienced physical or sexual abuse. These children, more than any, need to know what good, positive, safe touch looks like. They may have no concept of positive touch. It is doing further injury to continue to deprive them of the healthy touch they so desperately need.

Build touch into your day. Rub your child's back at bedtime. Give your child a hug in the morning or after school. Come up with a special handshake. Use high-fives indiscriminately. Rock your child if appropriate. Put your hand on your child's shoulder. Playfully tickle your child (as long as this doesn't cause distress). Engage in games involving touch, such as clapping games. Do what you can to provide safe, positive touch every day. This may sound overly simplistic, but it is very, very helpful in developing the attachment between a parent and an attachment-injured child.

It is important, of course, to be sensitive to your child's response to touch, and it is important to create a high level of safety around touch. Never force touch upon your child. If your child is shy of touch, you can set up a procedure of asking permission, e.g., "can I give you a hug?" "Is it OK if I put my hand on your shoulder?" Always respect their answer, letting them have control of this aspect of their life. Likewise, don't insist that they hug or give kisses to relatives, or anyone else. Who they share physical affection with should be something that is under their control.

It may also be helpful to state very directly to your child that, in your home, you only use and allow safe, positive touch. It not only allows for safety for your child but also allows you to redirect your child if they become physically aggressive.

If your child is new to your home, ease into touch, go slowly, starting with less threatening touch, such as high fives or playing a clapping game. Attachment-based games, discussed later in this chapter, can be an excellent way to introduce and provide touch in a non-threatening way.

The importance of touch for attachment healing cannot be overemphasized. Every day should include positive touch. Touch is nonverbal communication, and, since much attachment injury is preverbal, it can reach and heal the most injured, vulnerable part of your child.

If your child uses touch in a controlling or aggressive way, for example, hugging too hard or too long, you can instruct to appropriate touch. If they won't release the hug appropriately, teach them a 3-second hug. That is, hug, count for 3 seconds, release. If they give hugs, high fives, or other touches too roughly, practice gentle, appropriate touch with them. Have them practice until they can do it gently and appropriately. If they are likely to ambush you, running up on you and grabbing or bowling you over, or jumping on, or hugging tightly, then the rule needs to be to ask permission before touch. Again, coach and model for them. Provide praise for success, e.g., "Good Job," "Nice Hug," "Perfect!"

If your child is physically clingy in a way that makes you want to pull away, actively moving towards them with touch can help them gain the security they need to reduce the clinginess. They may be stuck in a pattern of clinginess that leads to rejection, which leads to more clinginess. You want to shift this dynamic. If you are proactive in giving touch, rather than reactive and pulling away, it will likely create this shift. It is also OK to set limits if needed, as long as you are providing good, regular, healthy touch.

Eye Contact

Another non-verbal conduit for connecting is eye contact. Think about the occasions in the supermarket when you have seen a young child with their parent, and the child makes eye contact with you... and just looks at you. They may look down and back up, or look to their parent then back to you. Eye contact precedes verbalizations as a way of connecting.

In the hectic world we live in, it can be easy to go the whole day without making eye contact with your child. If you find this is the case for you, make a concerted effort to build eye contact into your day and your interactions with your child.

It is common for the attachment-injured child to avoid eye contact or use it only for expressing anger or control. The healthy young child uses eye contact with a parent for safety and reassurance. They will visually check back with a parent in an uncertain or strange situation.

Developing eye contact with your child will support attachment. You can usually get a child to look at you if you use a positive, upbeat tone of voice and say, "look at me." And when they look at you, smile. This can be useful for just connecting, or when you want to communicate something to your child and want to make sure they are paying attention. Eye contact can be encouraged but should never be forced. Never insist on eye contact when you are angry. The "YOU

LOOK AT ME WHEN I TALK TO YOU!" statement is not useful. Your child has to experience eye contact as positive in order to make connecting safe.

One way to build eye contact into your day is through games. Peek-a-boo, eye blink games, and staring contests are some examples. These are attachment-based games, which will be discussed in the section on attachment-based play in this chapter. Additionally, Appendix A lists attachment-based play activities, and those that encourage eye contact are identified.

Mirroring

Mirroring facilitates attunement between you and your child. Mirroring is matching movements, posture, words, and sounds with your child. Parents and infants naturally mirror each other in their interactions and play. Imagine a parent and an infant interacting. Notice how they copy one another, smiling back and forth, making faces, and mimicking each other's vocalizations.

When a parent mirrors their child, it gives the child a felt sense of being seen, acknowledged, noticed, and creates attunement between parent and child. Children mirroring their parents is one of their primary ways of learning and growing. For instance, children learn to talk through listening and copying what they hear. Parents who talk to their babies are supporting their child's language development.

Sometimes gently copying your child's posture can create a subtle connection. For instance, suppose your child is sitting on the floor playing with dinosaurs. You can sit near them on the floor in the same way before engaging. You can also mirror or match your child's tone of voice. If they are speaking softly, speak softly back to them. If they are speaking enthusiastically, match that enthusiasm in your tone.

One of the easiest and most direct ways to provide mirroring for your child is through attachment-based play.

Many attachment-based play activities, such as follow-the-leader, clapping, and rhythm games, provide mirroring for your child. See Appendix A.

Singing and Rhythm

Singing and rhythm are regulating, soothing, and nurturing. It is one of the classic ways parents communicate comfort and love to their infant. The use of lullabies and rocking to soothe young children is common throughout the world.

Rhythm and singing are regulating. That is, they can help your child's nervous system to calm. By engaging in a rhythmic pattern with your child, such as clapping a rhythm together, your child gets to learn how to calm and regulate themselves with the help of an adult. This is called co-regulation.

Rhythm and singing can be integrated into play activities that also utilize touch, eye contact and/or mirroring. Examples include clapping games and Row Row Row Your Boat. Words to well-known children's songs can be changed to focus on positive messages to the child. Singing activities can be used to meet the child's need for nurturing.

Sing to your child. Rock your child. Dance with your child. Play drums with your child. Clap rhythms with your child. See Appendix A for attachment-based play activities using singing and rhythm.

Fun and Play

When you and your child are playing, laughing, and having fun together, attachment healing is occurring. At that moment, your child is not in shame or fear. Taking a playful attitude with your child can be extremely helpful in building connection and reducing defensiveness. It can also relieve tension and open up space for more positive experiences.

If ninety-nine percent of your time with your child feels like a struggle, it can be hard to shift the momentum of that experience, and easy to be in a mental framework of struggle any time you interact with your child, which closes down the potential for fun or a positive experience.

See if you can notice moments of ease or, better yet, moments of fun with your child. If you have moments of fun with your child, letting them know that you enjoyed that moment or that it was fun for you can help build connection and shift the story. Don't make a big deal of it because that may trigger resistance. Just mention it:

"Ah, that was fun! Thanks for coming with me."
"I noticed we got along well today!"
"Thanks for playing!"
"I had fun with you!

What you focus on will, hopefully, increase.

Attachment-Based Play

Attachment-based play is a powerful tool in addressing attachment injuries. It brings together touch, eye contact, singing/rhythm, and mirroring in a playful way. It is probably the easiest way to incorporate these elements into your child's life and the least likely to evoke defensiveness or resistance.

What is Attachment-Based Play?

Play has been described as the language of childhood, and so it is an ideal vehicle for communicating with children. There are varying definitions of attachment-based play. Attachment-based play is based on the earliest interactions between a parent and child. Attachment-based play is defined here as play between a child and primary caregiver that includes one or more of the following elements: touch, eye contact, mirroring, and/or singing/rhythm. Think about Peek-A-Boo, This Little Piggy, clapping games and rhymes and lullabies.

The most important purpose of attachment-based play is to heal attachment injuries through the experience of being cared for and engaged. All the talk in the world cannot take the place of attachment-based play. How many people, both child and adult, can say they know something in their head, but they don't feel it? By using play that includes touch, eye contact, mirroring, and song and rhythm with your child, they can have the physical experience of being loved and valued. This replicates the early experiences that support the development of those parts of a young child's brain related to attachment and relationship. You can engage the non-verbal parts of your child's brain through attachment-based play.

To support attachment, the play must include at least one of the four elements: touch, eye contact, mirroring, and song/ rhythm, and be interactive between caregiver and child. Other definitions of attachment-based play may differ from the one provided here, but this is what I have found to be most effective.

How to Implement Attachment-Based Play

Attachment-based play does not have to be very long, maybe 5 to 10 minutes for an older child, perhaps longer for a younger child. Gauge your child's interest and engagement. Some children will want to engage in this kind of play longer than others. The play can be very informal or part of a more structured playtime. A game of This Little Piggy or peek-a-boo can be snuck in between other activities. Attachment-based play will be most helpful to your child if you can engage consistently. If you can make it daily, so much the better.

Remember that attachment-based play is supposed to be fun, so bring enthusiasm and a playful attitude with you. If your child is resistant or avoidant, gently tickle them, or sing them a song, or play peek-a-boo. Keep the mood positive, then give it a break.

If you are engaged in therapy with your child that utilizes attachment-based play, it should be easy to transfer the play to the home.

You may be thinking, my child is too old for this! In fact, though your child may be older, or just act older, if they struggle with attachment injuries, they are likely emotionally young. Though focused on children 5 to 12, I have actually used attachment-based play in therapy for youth as old as 16 with their parents. I have yet to find a child who will not engage in a clapping game with their parent. Of course, you can modify which activities you choose based on the age of your child. Attachment-based play is generally regressive; that is, the child is allowed to be younger than their physiological age.

Don't worry if your child does not go along at first. You don't need to try to make your child participate. Just be playful with it. If you have a parenting partner or other adult known to your child, you can engage enthusiastically together in the play, periodically inviting your child to join. If your child chooses not to engage at all, give it a break and try again at another time or day. Be persistent.

Sometimes parents are skeptical that their child will want to engage in the attachment-based play at all or ever. They may believe their child will feel it is too babyish. I have yet to find that to be the case. Attachment-injured children are usually quite drawn to attachment-based play because it meets a deep inner need.

Parents may also worry that if they let their child act younger, they will stay indefinitely in a regressed state. I have seen the opposite to be true. When children receive this younger type of nurturing, they seem to ultimately be able to mature more easily.

You do not need to schedule a specific time for this play. Why not do thumb wrestling or eye blink games while waiting at the dentist's office? Or you could sing an attachment-based song, really, any time at all. Or you could make attachment-based play the beginning of scheduled playtime with your child, as described in the section on child-led play.

Use the tools of fun and enthusiasm to engage your child. Don't give up if they do not immediately seem interested. As noted earlier, give it a break, or engage with another family member and invite your child in. Never try to force or coerce your child into the play. Don't use rewards or consequences. Just be playful and patient.

Some of the games, such as clapping games, have levels of complexity. Start with simple and move to more complex as your child gains mastery.

In games where you take turns, you want to help set the hierarchy and model for your child by going first. Your child then gets a turn. The goal is for your child to learn that you can be in charge, and it can be fun!

Repetition of games is not only OK; it is desirable! Do not feel like you need to have something new all the time. Familiarity brings comfort and mastery. Repetition creates stronger neural pathways. Gauge your child's interest and introduce new games periodically to keep things fresh.

Have fun! Stay positive and out of power struggles. Fun increases bonding and reduces shame. When your child is having fun, your child is not in shame, which allows them to be better able to connect with you.

Keep a positive tone of voice. Your voice tone should convey enthusiasm and fun! To see what this looks like, observe or imagine a well trained, experienced preschool teacher. Note the positive tone of voice the teacher uses to corral the children into circle time, "OK, It's circle time! Come sit on your mats!" Enthusiasm is conveyed, and the children are more likely to pay attention and comply.

Do not try to talk about or verbally process attachment-based play. The play is experiential and designed to address preverbal injuries. Trying to process the play verbally may move your child into an older state and out of the experience, and may also increase resistance.

Within attachment-based play, just as with an infant, the child can do no wrong. Set limits around aggression as discussed in the next section, and redirect any inappropriate behavior, but be playful and sensitive to your child's response.

Appendix A has a list of attachment-based games. You can also find attachment-based play activities online or in other resources. Always evaluate, however, if the activity described meets the criteria for attachment-based play as defined here, including at least one of the four elements: touch, eye contact, mirroring, singing/rhythm. All of the games in Appendix A meet these criteria.

What attachment-based play is <u>not</u> is board games, imaginative play, competitive games, or intellectual games. These types of play can be incorporated in child-led play, described later in this chapter.

What to do when...

If your child is having difficulty engaging, you can do activities such as singing attachment-based songs that do not require their active participation. You can also be playful with their resistance. For instance, if you try to engage them, and they hide their face, what a good opportunity to playfully play peek-a-boo. If they hide behind the couch, you can say playfully, "Where is Dale? Where did Dale go? Is he in the cabinet? (Check the cabinet.) No. Is he behind the curtains? Noooo. Is he behind the couch? Oh, I see a foot! Could that be Dale's foot? (Gently tickle the foot.) I think it is! I think that's Dale's foot! Ah, there he is! There's my Dale! (With a gentle tickle if they will accept it.) So glad I found my little boy!" or you could then sing an attachment-based song to them.

If your child lashes out aggressively, perhaps pinching or hitting, you can say something like, "Oh, gentle touch! Remember, gentle touch only in this house," and if they will let you, "let me show you," and take their hand and lead it through a gentle touch.

You can also coach them to use their words, "Use your words! Do you want me to stop? Say 'Stop'" and then give verbal reinforcement for using their words. If physical touch seems to be the problem, you may need to back off, slow down, and ask permission to touch. "Can I give you a little tickle?" Then respect your child's response.

If your child is highly reactive to touch, slow down, ask permission to touch, and give your child the option to opt-out of touch. There are many attachment-based play activities involving mirroring, eye contact, and singing and rhythm that do not involve touch. Perhaps start with those. Some touch, such as high fives and clapping games, are less intense or intimate than others. Try those first. See if your child prefers light or firm touch. If touch continues to be problematic for your child, consider the possibility of sensory integration issues, referring to an occupational therapist specializing in sensory integration if appropriate. Also, be sure autistic spectrum disorders have been ruled out.

If your child is especially reactive to you, take it slow and be patient. Having another adult or older child engage with you and your child may help act as a buffer. If you are seeing a therapist with your child, hopefully you are engaging in attachment-based play in-session, which can easily translate to in-home play. If not, and your child is not engaging with you in this way, it might be a good idea to find a therapist who has attachment-based play in their repertoire.

If your child becomes overly agitated/excited in the play, integrate more regulating/self-calming games such as rhythm games and breathing games. Also, stop/go games (like Fast/Slow Clapping in Appendix A) help a child learn to regulate after excitement. Try doing some quiet singing games, holding and rocking your child at the end of the play to help them regulate. You may find your child gets overactive standing up, so you may choose only sitting games for a while until your child has learned to regulate their energy level better. Use each play experience to determine what works best for your child. If a game seems too activating for your child, move on to another game.

Be patient and expect resistance. The more injured the attachment, the longer it may take for your child to relinquish control. It is not unusual for a child to go along at first but then go through a period of avoidance. This may be a sign that your child is getting too close for comfort and is a last-ditch effort to maintain distance and/or control. This is a sign of progress. Stay consistent and positive, and keep offering the play. This phase does not usually last long.

Reasons your child may not participate could be that they are unsure of the safety of the situation, they do not want to give up control, or they feel uncomfortable because they are beginning to attach. These first two often happen early on. The latter is likely to occur after you have had some positive playtimes and is actually a sign that the attachment-based play is working. Generally, a child will not hold out for long. Be sure to continue to invite attachment-based play. Do not make the mistake of discontinuing the play due to your child's reluctance.

If your child is very resistant or reactive to you, your easiest strategy will be to work with a therapist in this modality.

Child-Led Play

A lot of parenting resources recommend child-led play. Child-led play is simply play where you allow your child to take the lead in any kind of play, without judgment. In child-led play, you want to avoid any judgmental or evaluative statements. It can be helpful just to notice out loud what is happening, "You're drawing with the red crayon now," or, "Look how high you have stacked the blocks!" or, "you're feeding the baby (doll) now." This provides mirroring and communicates acceptance.

While child-led play is a way of connecting, it will not provide the healing potency or impact that attachment-based play does. It can, however, be helpful to do a combination of both.

A formula that I have found works very well for some parents when they have time set aside to play with their child is to start with two or three attachment-based games that they choose, then move to child-led play. You can say something to your child like, "We'll play my games first, then we'll play what you want to play." When the parent goes first, it preserves the appropriate parent/child hierarchy and also avoids any struggle in trying to switch from child-led to adult-led activities.

Communication

If your child feels heard, it will increase your connection and reduce friction. Try the following communication skills.

Reflective Listening

All you want to do in reflective listening is reflect back to your child what you heard, particularly listening for and reflecting any feeling you hear. The hard part in this is refraining from making any statement that confers evaluation or judgment, opinion, or even problem solving. Reflecting back what you hear from your child will open the door to more conversation.

For instance, suppose you pick up your child from school, and they tell you about a conflict they had with other children.
Child: "Suzy and Alonzo wouldn't play with me today!"
Parent: Ah, Suzy and Alonzo wouldn't play with you today!

This is usually enough for the child to continue the story. Sometimes a very open-ended question (as opposed to a yes or no question) can be helpful:

Parent: Tell me about that.

Empathy Statements

An empathy statement, which is simply a reflection of feeling, can also deepen the conversation and let your child know that you understand them.

Parent: That must have been (sad, hard, disappointing)!
Child: I hate them!
Parent: You are angry!

Curiosity

A sense of curiosity using "I wonder" or "I'm curious" can be a way to further the conversation without bringing up a lot of defensiveness from your child.

Parent: I'm curious how you handled that situation.
Child: I told them they were stupid and went to play with Monika instead.

Highlighting

Highlighting is being selective about what you reflect back or emphasize. Here you could focus on your child calling the other children stupid or your child going to play with someone else. In highlighting, you want to highlight, or reflect the more positive or adaptive responses, to reinforce them:
Parent: Oh, so you went to play with someone else! I wonder how that was.
Child: OK.

Parent: I'm curious, what did you and Monika play?
Child: We played horses.
Parent: How was that?
Child: OK, but Monika can be bossy.
Parent: Ah, Monika can be bossy, but you had fun anyway.
Child: Yeah.

Deep Empathy

You may have a hard time understanding where your child is coming from. Perhaps you had very different childhood experiences, or you feel you would never behave the way your child behaves. Empathy can be defined as understanding how you would feel in your child's situation. Deep empathy can be further defined as understanding how your child feels in that situation.

Deep empathy requires that you take yourself out of your own experience and into your child's. Perhaps under your child's anger is fear or anxiety. When your child says, "You hate me!" and you know this is the farthest thing from the truth, it can be tempting to argue with them or negate that idea. Instead, you can validate your child's feelings or experience without saying that it is true. This opens up the communication rather than shutting it down.

For instance, when your child says, "You hate me!" you can respond, with compassion, "Gosh, that would be so hard to feel like I hate you. I'm so sorry you feel that way. I can imagine how hurtful that would feel." Thus, you have acknowledged their experience without saying it is true and without negating or arguing.

You can then say what is true from your perspective, if it seems useful, using clear "I" statements and owning your own experience, i.e., "For me, when I look at you, I feel a lot of love. Sometimes I feel frustrated when you aren't following directions, but always I feel love for you."

More on Parent/Child Communication

Communication will be revisited in the chapters on reducing and addressing behavior, as how you communicate is fundamental to how you parent.

For more general information on communication with children, I refer you to the excellent, classic book, *How to Talk so Kids Will Listen and Listen so Kids Will Talk* by Adele Faber and Elaine Mazlish.

Maintaining/Re-Establishing Connection

More than most children, children with attachment injuries need to know you are there, that you will show up, that you will come back. They may be more likely than most to give up on the connection when there is a minor disconnect. It is up to you, the parent, to show up and reconnect.

Always Show Up

This is important for all children, but especially for children with attachment injuries. Attachment-injured children may have been disappointed by parents/caregivers many times in their lives. They may not expect you to show up when you say you will, or maybe even to show up at all.

If you say you are going to be there, be there. If you will be away from your child for a period, set up a plan and let them know how frequently and approximately when you will call them (e.g., every evening), then call. Even if your child does not have anything to say on the phone, even if they seem unhappy to disrupt what they were doing to talk to you, even if they do not seem happy to hear from you at all, call anyway and let them know that you are thinking about them and love them.

Of course, life does happen, and sometimes a parent cannot follow through due to emergency circumstances. In these instances, communicate with your child as soon as reasonably able. Apologize. Let them know that you wanted to be with them, and if you could have, you would have. If appropriate, reschedule.

Reconnect

You come home after an absence, and you find your child turns away from you and avoids eye contact. It might be tempting to move on to something else. Don't. Engage them playfully, tickle them gently or say playfully, "I'm gonna get you!" and embrace them in a big bear hug. Then tell them how much you missed them.

It's up to the parent to reconnect. For regular absences, such as school, set up some kind of a re-engagement ritual. It could be as simple as a high five, handshake, hug, or a "tell me about your day" routine.

Likewise, if there has been a break in the connection with your child due to their behavior, always come back and check back in.

Be Present

It is not possible, and not necessarily even desirable, to be fully present with another person 100% of the time. We all have many responsibilities and distractions. When you do take time to connect with your child, however, practice being fully present. Put aside all the distractions in your life for that time to be focused on your child, yourself, and your interactions.

If you find your mind wandering to the next thing you need to do, or that thing that happened this morning, gently bring it back to your child. Using your senses can help. Look at and see your child. Notice the way their eyes crinkle when they smile or their forehead creases when they are concentrating. Listen to what they are saying. Note the sound of their voice. Observe what they are doing. Engage them playfully when appropriate. Put aside your phone or other distractions for a while. Stay engaged.

If you are watching the clock, just waiting for when you can go on to the next thing, your child may sense it and may engage in clingy or attention-seeking behavior, or simply disengage themselves. The more present you can be with any of the strategies in this chapter, the more successful you will be.

A Note for Foster Parents and Other Temporary Caregivers

Unfortunately, many children do not have an adult committed to them for the long term. A child may be placed in your home for the short term, or perhaps you work in a shelter for abused and neglected children, a foster family agency, a treatment program, or another short-term setting. Alternately, you may be a teacher, coach, or choir instructor of a child with attachment difficulties.

You may question the wisdom of building connection or engaging in attachment-based play with a child when you are short term in that child's life. This is a legitimate concern, and you do want to minimize emotional distress by being clear about your role in the child's life and maintaining appropriate boundaries.

If you are going to be in the child's life for at least several months, consider that a child with no experience of positive attachment, with no template for a healthy relationship, is worse off than a child with even a temporary experience of a healthy relationship. Research suggests that even a temporary positive connection to an adult can increase resilience for a child. As adults, people can often point to a teacher, mentor, coach, etc., that was important in their lives. This support is particularly important if the child does not have support at home.

Also, the attachment-based play elements of safe touch, eye contact, mirroring, and song and rhythm are desperately needed by attachment-injured children and, when provided with appropriate boundaries, can be healing in and of themselves.

If the child has a primary caregiver, take care not to undermine that person. If appropriate to your role, support the primary caregiver and, if possible, join with them to help the child.

If the child is living with you temporarily, you can help set boundaries and expectations by identifying yourself as a "helper person" in the child's life. If you know for sure how long the child will be with you, you or their social worker should let them know. If the plan is for the child to be placed in a permanent placement, you can identify that you are a helper person for the child until their forever home is found. This sets a time frame and can later be used to distinguish between helper people and forever people in the child's life.

You will want to maintain appropriate boundaries based on your role in the child's life. If you are not their forever parent or caregiver, then keep to attachment-based play activities that would be appropriate peer to peer, such as clapping games and thumb wrestling. The age of the child is a factor as well. Holding and rocking a four-year-old would be more appropriate than a twelve-year-old in a non-permanent setting.

If the child lives with you, how you handle the transition from your home to another placement is very important. You want the child's story to be that they were cared for and valued during their time with you. One way is to spend time in the last week with the child honoring the child and the relationship. This may include going to a special meal together, having a celebration with others in the home, and/or creating cards for each other expressing appreciation. In this last instance, the card can become a transition object that the child can take with them.

You can also provide an additional transition object for the child. Giving an elaborate or expensive gift would be counterproductive, but a special little gift, such as a special stone or other object, as a symbol of your time together, can serve as a nice reminder. One strategy for reducing the potential for distress at the possible loss of the object is to tell the child that the object represents the child's specialness and good wishes for them, and, even if someday they lose or misplace the object, it will not matter because the specialness and good wishes will still be there.

If the child has worked on behavior while in the home, the child should also be acknowledged for any progress and successes. In some instances, the closure could be likened to a successful graduation.

Don't hesitate to make genuine statements of caring and good wishes for the child:

> I am really going to miss you! I have enjoyed our time together and getting to know you. I am very excited and happy for you, though, because I know you are going to a home where you will get the care that you need and deserve!

For older children, if you feel the child has made a positive attachment, you can use this as a reference point for the child saying something like:

> I feel like we have developed a good relationship. I feel like we respect and care about each other. This is good because now you know what this feels like to be in a good relationship. Although all relationships are different, you'll be able to know if a relationship feels like a good relationship.

The child may ask questions like, "Why can't I live with you forever?" or, "Can you adopt me?" This may be a sign of a genuine attachment or indiscriminate attachment. Regardless, the answer can be the same. After validating the child's feelings, the answer can focus on your limitations and that the child deserves more. A possible response:

> You would like to live with me forever. I appreciate that! I sure have enjoyed our time together. I'm afraid that I am only a helper person in your life, though. I'm not able to be there for you all the time. You deserve a forever home and someone who can be there for you all the time (if this is the plan for the child). You need and deserve more than I can give you.

It is also important to acknowledge and validate underlying feelings and how hard goodbyes can be.

Make a Plan

What are some ways you would like to try to build connection with your child? Be as specific as you can.

1._____

_____

2._____

_____

3._____

_____

4. _____

_____

5. _____

_____

7

A New Story

We discussed how children with attachment injuries develop a rigid template or story of relationship that only allows them to see and recognize things that fit within that story. They will often misinterpret events to fit the maladaptive narrative. In this chapter, we will discuss ways that you can help them change that story.

Re-Storying

Many of the ideas for re-storying derive from Narrative Therapy concepts. The idea is that the child has created a storyline for their life based on their interpretation of events. This storyline then invests new events with the same meanings and themes of the maladaptive or dominant storyline. Any events that do not fit into the original or dominant storyline are often simply not seen or noticed.

For instance, a child who was abused or neglected when young may have created a storyline that goes something like: I was a bad kid, so people hurt me and no one loved me; I am still bad, and people (parents) are hurtful, so no one will ever love me, they will only hurt me. The child may not be conscious of this theme or storyline, and yet they act from it. One can see how this storyline or theme would create difficulties for the child in attaching to a caregiver.

It is also easy to see how this child might become easily emotionally dysregulated; the child sees themselves as bad, which creates intolerable feelings of shame and anxiety. It does not take much to trigger these difficult feelings (shame, hurt, anger) and push the child beyond their ability to cope. Contributing to this is the fact that the child's coping/self-soothing skills are often minimal due to their early history.

Furthermore, if a child feels they are bad, they will do bad things, even when not dysregulated, creating a lot of discipline challenges. Then, if a caregiver tries to discipline the child, the child will interpret it as, "I'm bad" and, "They are trying to hurt me (with the discipline)." It will be very difficult for the child to see that the caregiver is trying to help them through discipline or consequences; therefore, a vicious cycle develops.

The underlying dominant, maladaptive story should be addressed in therapy, but there are things you can do outside of therapy to help shift the story.

Positives in the Moment

It is always useful to highlight or notice positives in the moment, particularly conveying that you are enjoying your child's company. It does not have to be over the top. In fact, for attachment-injured children it is usually better to be low key. Some examples:

"This is fun!"
"Thanks!"
"I appreciate your help with that."

"Good for you!"
"Nice!"

or non-verbally:

high five
thumbs up
fist bump

Anything that conveys that you are enjoying your child's company can help. With repetition over time, a new story will be supported.

A Time When...

Here you want to develop the history of positive relational experiences by focusing on relationship questions. As has been noted, attachment-injured children may ignore events that do not fit into a negative, maladaptive narrative. In this exercise, you are bringing a different story of relationship to your child's awareness.

Topics should be relationship-based and focused on positive experiences. You can go back as far in time as you want, or as recent as you wish. By varying your answers in time, you eventually create a new storyline or narrative. You can also extend the story into the future with things you look forward to. This future question can also be near term or long term future. Some sample questions:

A time we had fun together
A time when we got along well
Something we are proud of each other for
Something we wish for each other
Something we did for each other
An appreciation for each other

A time we laughed together

Something we are looking forward to doing with each other

You can also come up with some questions of your own and rotate through them, one or two at a time. If you like, you could write the questions on separate cards and have your child pick a card to start the process. Focus on the relationship and appreciations, as in the above questions, to change the story of self and relationship over time to a more positive one.

This can be done daily or weekly. It is fine to repeat questions. Remember, repetition is good! It can be a very nice thing to do at night as part of the bedtime routine, perhaps as the last thing before sleep, or maybe a way of closing playtime with your child. It doesn't have to be scheduled, however, nor does it need to be long. In fact, it can be quite short. If you do this regularly, the repetition will create an impact.

Highlight Reel

At any point in the day, you can review highlights. You can also make this part of something you do at dinner, or bedtime, or some other specific time. When you do so, talk about concrete specifics and highlight any positives. Emphasize any times that you had fun, or that you, as parent/caregiver, were helpful to your child, or that your child was helpful to you. Being descriptive and using concrete details are important because this brings your child back into the positive experience in a way that is not likely to bring up a negative reaction. Be matter of fact. This helps your child develop an ongoing narrative that is positive and reality-based.

For instance:

Remember we went to the store this morning? And we saw Shira and her mom at the store too. And we bought apples and milk and bread. What else did we buy?...

That's right, we bought peanut butter and jelly too. Remember when your shoe fell off? That was funny, huh? Then you put your shoe on all by yourself, and I helped you tie your shoe. We worked well together...

How much detail you put in and how you phrase it may depend on your child's developmental level. Things you want to highlight are:

- moments you were getting along
- moments you had fun
- times you were helpful to your child
- times your child was helpful to you

You may also ask your child to share what positives they remember about the day. If they bring up a difficult event, acknowledge it, talk about how it resolved, then pivot to more positive events:

Child: You wouldn't let me buy a candy at the story, and I got mad!
Parent: You got mad when I wouldn't let you get a candy! (reflective listening). But then you calmed down. How did you calm down? (curiosity).

A child may not have an answer here. In that case, you might prompt:

Parent: Did you think about something else, or take a deep breath, or just forget about it?
Child: I guess I just forgot about it.
Parent: So eventually, you forgot about it, and you were OK.
Child: I'm still mad!
Parent: You are still mad! OK. Can you tell me something about today that you liked?

If your child can't come up with anything positive, you can describe a positive or neutral moment. By providing details, you bring your child, in their mind, back to that more positive experience, which may help them move on.

Storytime

Throughout history, stories have been used to gently teach and instruct. The human mind seems to use stories to organize and make sense of the world. So why not tell your child stories that speak to connection and positive parent/child interaction? Most children enjoy being read to, and study after study has shown that reading to your child furthers their cognitive development. Why not read books that will also further their ideas about relationship?

I have used a number of picture books with parents and children. You may feel that picture books are too young for your child, but, most likely, your child is at a younger emotional age than chronological age. Picture books have the advantage of being engaging, short, and to the point. I have used picture books with children as old as 12 years and their parents.

In Appendix B: Resources, you'll find a list of some of my favorite picture books that explore the enduring bond between parent and child. Perhaps read them regularly to your child, or slip them in now and then. Remember that repetition is good. It helps re-train the brain.

Talk About Your Child

Parents are often told not to talk about their child in front of them. When parents are talking about them, children are listening! Talking about your child in their hearing, however, can be put to good use. If you want to help change your child's self-image to be more positive, how you talk about them can be useful.

Think about the qualities and behaviors in your child you would like to highlight, and the next time you are on the phone with a friend or family member, and your child is in hearing distance, mention it.

For instance, your friend calls and asks how your day is going. Your child is in the room. Perhaps you and your child had a good moment this morning when you went to the park. Maybe later, your child had a temper tantrum. While your child is listening, you have a choice of what you mention to your friend. If you need to vent or process the temper tantrum, take the standard advice and do not do it while your child is anywhere in earshot (you can do this another time). Instead, focus on the positive moment:

"Well, Janie and I had a great time going to the park this morning." Now, your child will be listening and is expecting you to say, "but...." and discuss her misbehavior. Don't do it. Add some specific details, "we played on the swings and built a castle in the sand. We brought a lunch of peanut butter and jelly sandwiches." Mention any other positives, then leave the subject and go on to other topics with your friend.

Make sure that what you say is true. Don't paint a rosy picture when the picture was anything but! This will only confuse your child. Even if it was a difficult day, you will probably be able to find some highlight, some exception to the rule, when you had a pleasant moment with your child. If you can't, then don't discuss it at all in front of your child.

Alternately, perhaps your child had a temper tantrum but did a much better job getting themselves under control. Focus on the latter, rather than the former: "Janie is also getting better and better at handling big feelings. I'm very proud of her!"

All children are cooperative at times. Highlight these times when you talk to others about your child. If you have a parenting partner, you can strategically plan to talk about your child within their hearing in positive ways.

Do remember that your child is always listening, and avoid, at all costs, talking to others negatively about your child in your child's hearing. You don't want to sabotage all your good work by making an offhand comment to someone. Don't, even affectionately, nickname or call your child "a little monster" or similar; or, when they are doing exceptionally well, don't say, "What did you do with my child?!" or "Who is that child?!" implying that the behaving child is not your child, or that your child wouldn't behave. This just reinforces their already negative story about themselves. Your words may be written in sand to you, but they can be written in stone to your child.

Your Child's Story

In Multi-Modal Attachment Therapy (M-MAT), there is a major intervention called an attachment narrative in which the therapist works with the parent and child in a re-telling of the child's story. The goal is to re-tell the story in a healthy, adaptive way, correcting ideas of blame and responsibility. This is most easily done with a therapist in the therapy session where there is professional support.

There are times, however, when your child's history may come up in conversation. In these instances, simply using reflective listening and empathetic statements, as described in chapter 6, is an excellent strategy. Keep in mind that sometimes it is enough just to be heard, and you do not have to "fix" anything for them. Feeling heard can be both healing for your child and help your child to connect positively to you.

You can also try helping your child re-story by focusing on any or all of the following:

• **The child is not at fault** - Children carry a lot of shame and responsibility for things that happen to them when they are little, particularly related to their parent's behavior. Young children naturally feel that the things that happen around them, especially when they involve their parents, are their fault. It has to do simply with the way a very young child's brain works. If they have happy, positive early experiences, it gives them a positive sense of self and a sense of efficacy, or effectiveness, in the world. As discussed in previous chapters, if they have negative experiences, they feel they are to blame, or there must be something wrong with them. They harbor the belief that they are bad, otherwise these things would not have happened to them.

If it comes up in conversation, these core beliefs can be addressed both directly and indirectly. It is OK to say to your child, "You know, that wasn't your fault. It is never the child's fault when a grown-up (hurts them, leaves them, drinks too much, does drugs, etc.). Little kids are just little kids. Grown-ups are responsible for their own behavior."

Sometimes the child feels that abuse is their fault because they did something wrong, i.e., misbehaved or talked back. You can tell your child something to the effect of, "Even if a child did something wrong, it's not OK for grown-ups to hurt the child. They should help teach them, but not hurt them."

Children often feel that domestic violence between adults is their fault. Sometimes this may be exacerbated by the fact that the domestic violence started with an argument about the child. You can tell your child, "Grown-ups need to learn to use their words to work things out. It doesn't matter how an argument started; a child is never responsible for grown-ups behavior. Just like we are teaching you to use your words when you are upset, grown-ups need to use their words too..."

Children often feel responsible for a parent's substance abuse problem. They think if they were better children, their parents would not have used. Sometimes parents may have reinforced this idea by telling their child that they are "too much" or they can't handle them. This is probably best addressed in therapy, but if it comes up, it is OK to say something like, "Ah, that wasn't your fault. There is nothing you did that caused that problem."

- **Empathy, validation, and normalization of your child's feelings** - Your child may not be able to express their feelings. It is OK to say things like: "That could be so hard for a little kid" or, "Gosh, that must have been so confusing." This allows children to better understand their experiences and feelings and to continue to share.

- **How things are different now** - Discuss how things are different now from how they were then, particularly around safety. Asking questions with a focus on safety is a good way to do this. "That was scary! That wasn't very safe. How are things different now? How are they safer now?"

Discuss how things are different now/why your child is safe now. This can include parent (we will never hurt you), child (you are bigger now and can get help), and situational (there is always food in the house) changes. This helps reduce anxiety and changes the story from "I am not safe" to "I am safe." You might ask your child questions such as, "What do we do to make sure everyone is safe?" "How are things different now than they were then?" You can both elicit, reinforce and offer answers, "That's right, Mommy and Daddy don't do drugs." Sometimes leading questions are appropriate, "Do we always make sure that there is good food in the house?" "That's right! We always have good food to eat!"

Reinforce your child's agency in being able to be safer, "You are bigger now, and you have words so you can always tell mom and dad if there is a problem. We will always help you."

Take care not to push for answers that everything is good now, and everything was bad then. There may have been positives in their early story that are important to them. For instance, they may have had siblings or cousins or others that they were positively connected to that they are no longer in contact with, or they may have had some fun experiences that they remember fondly. You do not need to comment on these experiences except to reflect back what you hear, "Oh, that sounds like fun," or, "Sounds like your sister was important to you."

Also, there may be things currently that they do not like. For instance, they may have enjoyed eating candy whenever they wanted, but now can no longer do so. Or, maybe they don't like having to go to bed at an earlier time. For situations like these, let them know you understand their feelings and ask them why they think that it is different in their home now. If they can't generate it themselves, explain the rationale for these changes, always letting them know that you have their best interest at heart, "I know it seems fun to stay up as long as you want, but it is important for children to get good sleep so they can be healthy and happy. It is important to me that you are healthy and well."

Never ever put down your child's biological parents, family or early caregivers. To do so is to put your child down and will harm, rather than help, their self-esteem.

Make a Plan

What are some strategies you would like to implement to help your child re-story? Be as specific as you can.

1._____

_____

2._____

_____

3._____

_____

4. _____

_____

5. _____

_____

8

Attachment-Based Therapy

If your child suffers from moderate to severe attachment injury, then therapy is essential. (Full disclosure: I'm a therapist!). The type of therapy is equally important. I have had many parents and children come to me after several years of therapy without any significant change for the better. It was not necessarily that the therapy received was not a good or established therapy, but rather, it was not a match for their attachment-injured child. It would be like going to an allergist to address diabetes. The treatment needs to fit the underlying concerns.

Why is Therapy Important?

You may be a do-it-yourselfer, I know I am, and be wondering, can't I do this myself? If I provide the proper parenting, do I need a therapist for my child? If your child has significant attachment injuries, I would say a therapist is needed, for the following reasons:

- Due to the very nature of attachment injuries, your child is likely to be highly reactive and resistant to you, their parent or caregiver. Intervention by a neutral third party can be extremely helpful and may be absolutely necessary. I have had children that initially could not tolerate being in the therapy room with their parents, becoming quickly highly agitated and reactive. As an intermediary, I was able to help these children be receptive and facilitate connection between parent and child in a way that would not otherwise have been possible.
- A therapist will be able to have perspective that a parent cannot. I had a friend who was a therapist and had worked with children with challenging behaviors for years. She told me that when she adopted, she did not believe that she would need to have a therapist for her and her child, but she was wrong. It is hard to have perspective with our own children.
- A therapist has specialized training and should have skills to help your child, and help you help your child.
- It takes a village. A child with significant attachment injuries needs a lot of support, and so do you! I know, you are a tough, strong person and parent. Maybe you feel that, maybe you don't. Regardless, a knowledgeable therapist can provide a tremendous amount of support in understanding and helping your child. They can also be a listening ear, validating your experiences in a way that perhaps a partner or friend cannot. If you feel part of a team, have someone you can share your frustrations with and who can walk you through some of the parenting challenges, life with your child will feel much easier.
- Therapy can work! A really good attachment-based therapy can be effective in helping your child connect to you, become the person you know they can be, and reach their full potential. Of course, each situation is different, each child is different, and no therapy has a guaranteed outcome in any particular case. Nevertheless, I have seen a lot of children

become healthy young people using attachment-based therapy. Multi-Modal Attachment Therapy (M-MAT) is the therapy model I developed and use, but there are other models as well, which will be discussed further in this chapter.

The Failure of Traditional Therapies with Attachment-Injured Children

To understand what to look for in therapy for your child, it is helpful to look at why some child therapy models don't work.

Traditional child therapies such as behavior therapy or interventions, non-directive play therapy, Cognitive Behavioral Therapy (CBT), and skills-based therapies have their place in the world of child therapies but, unfortunately, are not particularly useful or effective with attachment-injured children.

The child's poor understanding of relationship and impaired cause and effect reasoning are largely responsible for why they do not respond well to traditional behavioral interventions. In fact, behavioral interventions can make the child worse because the child will interpret consequences as another injustice done to them, consistent with the initial narrative of their lives, and positive reinforcers as an attempt to control them. Positive reinforcers, often treats, desired objects, or privileges, sometimes do not work at all because the child's perceived need for control far outweighs the reward.

An attachment-injured child may view a behavior plan as an attempt to control them, and giving up control, in their worldview, is dangerous. Other times the child may comply temporarily to obtain the reinforcer, but then fall right back into previous behavior because the forces driving the behavior are still present.

For behavioral interventions to work, the child must believe, deep down, that the caregiver has their best interest at heart and must be able to connect their behavior to consequences and rewards in a cause and effect manner. If not, behavioral interventions become a game and a power struggle between child and caregiver. If the child cannot rebel directly, the child may become sneaky and get back at the caregiver in sneaky or passive-aggressive ways.

For example, when a parent tries to give their child a time out in their room for behavior, the child may have little sense that they created the time out by their behavior. Rather, they believe the parent is being 'mean' and does not like them, which generates anger, hurt, and the continued belief that they are bad, further generating extreme and difficult behavior.

If the parent uses a reward system, the child may feel that the parent is trying to control them. They may go along until they get the desired reward and then act out, or, if they do not earn the reward, they again may feel the parent is being mean to them. Alternately, the reward may have little meaning for them at all. The child's interpretations, of course, are consistent with the narrative through which they organize all of their experiences. Events inconsistent with the original narrative are either not noticed or misinterpreted. Thus, despite the parents' best efforts, the child gets worse over time rather than better.

I have heard a teenage youth state, with genuine anger and hurt, that, when they were little, their parents removed all their toys from their room, only to share a moment later in the conversation that they routinely broke and threw their toys. They had not really connected the one with the other. Or, with deep hurt, a youth may relay that their parents took away all their privileges at a time when they were completely out of control, running the streets, doing drugs, lying, and disobeying all household rules. The hurt that they feel comes from their earliest sense of abandonment, fear, and anger, the only lens through which they are able to view their later experiences. Therefore consequences, both natural and otherwise, feel like just another hurt that their parent or the world is inflicting upon them, strengthening an already negative worldview.

Another traditional child therapy is non-directive play therapy. In non-directive play therapy, the child is largely left to their own devices with minimal structure and direction from the therapist. The therapist provides reflective and mirroring responses. This can be an effective therapy for many children and many situations. For the attachment-injured child, however, this too closely mirrors their earliest experiences of neglect. The child is still alone. The child is still without limits and structure and an adult to help make sense of their world. The mirroring and reflective responses that the therapist provides are not harmful, but they are not usually enough to break through the initial narrative.

Sometimes, in non-directive play, the attachment-injured child will move away from open-ended imaginative play because it is too anxiety-provoking. Sometimes the child will repeat a theme over and over again in a way that appears stuck. Other times, the child will be very controlling of the therapist in the play session, telling them what to do in every instance. And sometimes, the child will enact in play a high level of violence that is repetitive, feels counterproductive, and never seems to get resolved.

I have had many parents bring their children to me after months or even years of therapy that has not succeeded in bringing about any significant positive change. The child is injured in the area of relationship; it is through relationship that the child needs to be healed. Hands-off, non-directive play therapy is insufficient in these circumstances. If healing occurs in this context, it is most likely due to the therapeutic relationship, but this is a long, long road. It is possible that a mildly attachment-injured child with a non-directive play therapist could make some improvement over many years with the therapist. It would likely be the safe, stable, long term relationship, however, that is providing the greatest impact.

Far more often, this therapy fails to address the child's needs altogether.

Cognitive Behavioral Therapy (CBT) and skills-based therapies (e.g., self-soothing skills, communication skills) are useful when integrated into a larger attachment-based therapy but, by themselves, fall short with the attachment-injured child. This is because these therapies primarily address issues from a cognitive, verbal perspective. Much of attachment injury is preverbal and body-oriented. We know young children need touch, eye contact, and play, all nonverbal avenues of growth, for appropriate development and attachment.

Also, for CBT and skill-building based therapies, attachment-injured children often will not cooperate. If they do cooperate in the session and learn some skills, they often will not apply them in real-life situations. They hold the beliefs that their parent is trying to hurt them and that they are bad, so they have no motivation to get their anger or behavior under control. Their anger and acting out may be the only sense of power and control they have in their lives, and they are unwilling to give that up. They need to both change their underlying beliefs and begin to experience a positive attachment before the skill building can be effective.

Yet another approach to helping these children is medication. It is not unusual for attachment-injured children to be on any number of medications to help them to calm, to focus, and/or to reduce depression, anxiety, and other symptoms. For some children, medication seems to be helpful in conjunction with therapy, and a psychiatric referral is often in order. For no attachment-injured child, however, is medication alone the answer. A relational injury requires a relational remedy. Of course, symptoms of children with attachment injuries are often complex, and a thorough evaluation by a child psychiatrist can be very useful.

In summary, children with attachment injuries have been challenging to help due to their rigid core beliefs or worldview.

Many traditional child therapies have their place and can be integrated into effective therapy, but only when attachment is put center stage in the therapy process.

Important Components of Attachment-Based Therapy

The following, I feel, are the necessary components for an effective therapy addressing attachment injuries:

- The relationship between you and your child is front and center. The primary focus of the therapy must be on relationship development. Everything else is secondary.
- Positive, healthy touch is an element of relationship building in the therapy.
- Attachment-Based Play is used as a modality for creating connection.
- There is a means to re-story your child's life in a way that is adaptive and helpful to your child.

Other beneficial components:

- Skill building to address skills deficits (specifically in self-calming/self-soothing, feelings identification and expression, communication, boundaries and social skills).
- Parent support - individual sessions with parents to support parenting, provide emotional support, work on developing a support system, address behavior concerns, and provide crisis management and safety planning.

What to Avoid

• Any therapy that does not focus on the parent/child relationship.
• Any therapy that includes only the child. Although, if the child is extremely reactive to their parent, it may be useful for the therapist to have a couple of sessions with the child individually to develop rapport so that they can be more effective in the joint sessions.
• Any therapy in which the child is coerced or shamed into participating. This may seem obvious, but there have been previous "attachment therapies" that have been coercive or shaming in nature.
• Any therapist that undermines you in front of your child, blames or shames you, or doesn't seem to understand attachment injuries. You want a therapist who can help you parent your child more effectively, without blame or shame.

Some Promising Therapies

In this section, I include therapy models that I feel have some use in addressing attachment injuries.

Multi-Modal Attachment Therapy (M-MAT)

This is a model developed by myself over years of working with attachment-injured children and their families. It incorporates aspects of Theraplay® and DDP (described below), and more (e.g., cognitive behavioral therapy, narrative therapy, and skills-based therapy). M-MAT includes all of the necessary and beneficial components of attachment-based therapy described previously in this chapter.

The primary focus of healing in M-MAT is relational. The goal of the therapy is to heal the attachment/relational injuries so the child can then access all the resources that healthy attachment allows within themselves, and with others, in order to reach their full potential as a human being.

M-MAT is a two-pronged approach with both a play and a talk component. The play component utilizes largely non-verbal forms of communication, connection, and nurturing, such as mirroring, rhythm, touch, and eye contact.

The talk component engages the power of language and the child's thoughts by addressing cognitive distortions, responsibility, and self-concept through re-storying, skill building, and psychoeducation, creating a new narrative in which the child can organize and make sense of their experiences in a healthy, adaptive way.

Together, the two components reinforce each other, allow for deeper integration and healing, and are far more powerful than either alone. Combined, they access many parts of the brain and harness the incredible healing power inherent in both left and right brain modalities. If we presume that the child with attachment injuries has parts of the brain that are underdeveloped, the parts associated with attachment and relationship, then the goal is to stimulate and develop these parts of the child's brain through experiences of play and talk.

M-MAT is a structured therapy, with each session having a specific beginning, middle, and end. It is geared towards children 5 to 12 years old but can be adjusted for younger or older children.

You can find more information at www.m-mat.org. Additionally, the book: *M-MAT Multi-Modal Attachment Therapy: An Integrated Whole-Brain Approach to Attachment Injuries in Children and Families* is available wherever books are sold.

Theraplay ®

This is an attachment-based play therapy between parent and child that has been around for a long time, and has good research to back it. For more information: www.theraplay.org

Dyadic Developmental Therapy (DDP)

This therapy, developed by Daniel Hughes, Ph.D., works with parent/child interactions in developing the relationship between parent and child. A key concept in this approach is PACE - Playfulness, Acceptance, Curiosity, and Empathy. For more information: www.ddpnetwork.org

Give it Time, but Not Too Much Time

No therapy is a magic bullet. All take some time. I ask parents to work with me for 10 sessions after the assessment period before making any decision about the therapy. I might suggest you give a therapist at least 12 sessions (treatment sessions, after assessment) to decide if the therapy is helpful.

Do not expect your child's attachment injuries to be resolved, but do expect at least the beginnings of change. Maybe your child is now cooperating in the therapy where they weren't before. Maybe your child, though still struggling, is a little more cooperative at home or is engaging you more positively. Maybe you are feeling the connection to your child, and your child's to you, more strongly. Look for positive change, and don't allow one bad day or bad moment to blind you to progress that is being made. Be aware that progress is often two steps forward, one step back, and also, as discussed in chapter 4, sometimes it will get worse before it gets better. But after 12 weeks, you should be noticing some shift.

If progress is being made, stick with it. Time is an essential factor in your child's healing. It takes time for trust and true connection to develop and to change the maladaptive story or narrative of your child's life.

If you are not noting any progress, or if your child is generally getting worse, talk with the therapist about your concerns. There may need to be an adjustment made in the therapy, or maybe a different therapy or therapist is needed.

How to Find a Therapist

Now that you are armed with information on attachment and what to look for in therapy, you are ready to find a therapist! First and foremost, you want to make sure they have an understanding of attachment and children. Look for therapists who list themselves as attachment or attachment-based therapists or M-MAT (Multi-Modal Attachment Therapy), DDP (Dyadic Developmental Psychotherapy), or Theraplay trained.

A lot of therapists throughout the United States list through Psychology Today. Regional professional organizations such as California Marriage and Family Therapists (CAMFT) also have listings. You can find DDP and Theraplay trained therapists through their respective organizations. Likewise, I am compiling a list of M-MAT trained therapists, which you can access by contacting me through my contact information listed in the back of this book or at www.m-mat.org.

Interview your prospective therapist. Ask them about their understanding of attachment and how they address this in the therapy. Ask about the therapy model they use. Go with your gut feeling.

9

Understanding Behavior

To address behavior effectively, it helps to have an understanding of behavior as related to attachment injuries.

Attachment-Injured Children and Behavior

While parents would like their children to behave because it is the right thing to do, many children, and especially attachment-injured children, are not that advanced in their thinking or moral development. For children with attachment injuries, fear, anger, anxiety, hurt, and low self-worth all contribute to lashing out. Poor impulse control and poor self-regulation can be contributing factors as well. These children may also be re-enacting abuse they experienced or observed in their early years.

Attachment-injured children are often run by two opposing forces: the need to connect and the fear-driven need to keep emotional distance. Negative behavior is one way to connect with caregivers through the caregiver's emotional response to the behavior, while at the same time maintaining or creating emotional distance. Sometimes the child's impulse to push away others can result in very hurtful behavior. It may be much more in keeping with the child's world view to accept an angry response from a parent rather than a loving response. It merely confirms what they already think they know: they are bad, and their parents don't love them.

In the worldview of a child with attachment injuries, they are not OK, and the people around them are not OK. Therefore, there is little motivation to behave. Also, the child may gain a strong sense of power by acting-out either aggressively or passive-aggressively, which further supports the problematic behavior. For attachment-injured children, this is a defense against the extreme powerlessness and fear they experienced when very young. It is not unusual to find that the whole household is run around the child's extreme behaviors. When that happens, it only feeds the maladaptive behavior.

Some of the most challenging behavior for parents to cope with may not be behavior that occurs during a temper tantrum (i.e., while the child is emotionally dysregulated) but rather, any apparently calculated, destructive, or hurtful behavior. For example, a child sneaking and breaking a parent's prize possession. To understand the behavior, we need only look at the consequences of the behavior. It likely pushes the parent away (creating emotional distance and, thus, a sense of safety) and angers the parent (creating a sense of power and control). The parent's response also establishes an emotional connection between child and parent, if even a negative one. So the behavior has served to create connection and a sense of power and control while simultaneously pushing away closeness.

It may also be the only way the child knows how to express anger or frustration. Perhaps the child is mad at their parent for setting a limit. They don't know how to say they are mad. They don't know how to express their frustration, and so they act-out. The anger may be amplified by the many real hurts they experienced at the hands of caregivers when younger. At that moment, they may actually be acting from a past hurt, triggered by a perceived current slight. Sneaky and passive-aggressive behavior, in particular, can be an indication that a child does not feel safe expressing difficult emotions and/or does not know how.

Attachment-injured children also may have had no structure, limits, or boundaries in the earliest part of their lives. If so, they can be like untamed beings with the expectation of doing what they want when they want. Thus, they may perceive any parental boundaries or limits as the parent wanting to unfairly control them.

Attachment-injured children do not readily take responsibility for their behavior. Of course, many children avoid responsibility for wrongdoing to avoid getting in trouble or due to feelings of guilt or shame. The attachment-injured child, however, may take this to an extreme. This may include lying when the evidence of their wrongdoing is incontrovertible (while their hand is still in the proverbial cookie jar). They may stick to their lie no matter what, blaming others and throwing a tantrum when caught or questioned.

This is likely a defense against intolerable feelings of shame they may feel when caught and/or the fear of getting in trouble. It is also possible that getting in trouble, when the child was very little, led to physical and/or verbal abuse, which may have been life-threatening, or perceived by the child as life-threatening. This denial of responsibility, therefore, can be a survival strategy. Anything associated with survival is more strongly held in the brain and nervous system and will likely take longer to change than other behavior.

A primary goal in parenting your child is to increase their tolerance and acceptance of positive attention through building connection and creating safety, and to move them away from negative behaviors.

Understanding Emotional Dysregulation

Extreme behavior may occur when your child is emotionally dysregulated. Emotional dysregulation means that emotions have overtaken thinking. The child is acting from the more primitive, emotional parts of the brain. Their body is flooded with stress hormones, and the frontal cortex, or reasoning part of the brain, is not being engaged.

Sometimes, no matter what you do or how well you parent, your child will become dysregulated. All children do, and many attachment-injured children do so more often, or for longer, or to more of an extreme than others. We generally call it a meltdown or temper tantrum.

Even as adults, we have all experienced becoming somewhat dysregulated, e.g., that time when you were so angry you did or said something you didn't mean or usually wouldn't do. Think about the energy you feel in your body at that moment. Adrenaline is up, and your body wants to move, wants to do something. It is a fight or flight response. At that moment, you are not thinking rationally. I, at least, have had the experience of feeling very angry yet thinking that I was thinking clearly. Later, after all the stress hormones are gone, I would find myself thinking of the situation in a completely different light. When you are emotionally dysregulated, it is very difficult to access the reasoning part of the brain, the frontal cortex.

The same thing happens to your child. Trying to reason with them when they are escalated or emotionally dysregulated is not generally effective. Talking about consequences at that moment will likely only further escalate them. The first thing you'll want to do is help them regulate or calm themselves.

In chapter 11: Addressing Behavior, you'll find a section on helping your child calm.

10

Reducing Challenging Behavior

First, a caveat: Some behavior is not preventable. Children will be children. They are learning how to regulate themselves and function in the world. Their brains are not fully developed, they have limited life experience, they are more subject to impulsive or reckless behavior, and they are more easily emotionally dysregulated. Any parent can tell you of experiences wherein they did everything "right," but their child had a complete meltdown.

All of this is just amplified with attachment-injured children, who may also have many unknown triggers from their early experiences and are acting from a dysfunctional view of the world and relationship. While a securely attached child, on some level, wants to please their parents and have their approval, a child with significant attachment injuries may not have that motivation.

Many parents I have worked with have been frustrated with parenting classes because the strategies do not work with their attachment-injured children. Traditional parenting strategies are designed for children who are attached to their parents. So the first step, then, is to build the relationship/attachment.

I have worked with families in therapy wherein once the attachment became more secure, behavioral issues, even extreme ones, resolved. That being said, you want to avoid exacerbating behavior, and there are things you can do, along with working on the attachment, that will help reduce behaviors and create a positive environment for attachment to grow. Working on behavior will help create a conducive environment for connecting to your child. Working on relationship-building and re-storying will help you successfully implement strategies for reducing and addressing behavior. The two work together.

Note that the "creating safety" strategies in chapter 5 can also help reduce behaviors as the safer your child feels, the more easily they will be able to manage themselves. The following are additional preventative measures that can help reduce challenging behavior and may, at times, keep it from escalating. The things listed below, along with the safety recommendations in chapter 5, can contribute to creating the space for the seeds of attachment to take root and flourish.

It is important to consider that as you make changes, your child is likely to test or resist. Thus, behavior may become worse before it becomes better. One common error is not sticking with the structure or strategies long enough. On one level, your child may be hoping you will give in. On a completely different level, I believe all children really want and need a competent adult to be in charge, no matter how much they protest. Don't let the injury-driven behavior win.

Structure and Environment

The environment you create and the structure you set can either exacerbate or reduce behaviors.

House Rules: Routine, Safety, Respect

Your child will do better if they know what is expected of them. Rules generally fall into three categories: routine, safety, and respect.

Routine includes things like bedtimes, hygiene routines, homework times, chores, etc. As parents, you should be setting the basic routines for the household. This provides a level of predictability and safety. It can be helpful for some children to have a chart somewhere with the daily routine laid out.

If your child has difficulty with a particular routine, such as getting ready for school, it may help to have a specific routine checklist written out and put somewhere where the child can easily access it. For younger children, pictures or icons can be helpful. This was a valuable strategy for one family where the parent felt they constantly had to prompt their child in the morning, leading to conflict and power struggles. Once the child was able to access a list, they were able to more successfully take care of their before school routine, and conflict was reduced.

Safety and respect are key requirements for any household or community, so these should be key rules. I once worked in a treatment program for children that had only 3 rules: Be safe, be respectful, and have fun. The first two rules were required; the third was optional. This worked out really well. Almost any misbehavior could be corrected by referencing the first two rules. The advantage of this approach is that the reason for the limit is evident. The staff might only have to say, "Ah, that's not respectful!" or, "Be Safe!" to redirect the child.

In your household, you may want to define these further. You can sit down with household members and discuss what it means to be respectful (e.g., not calling names, respecting things by using as intended, etc.). Parents can tell their children that they will always be respectful to them, and they expect the same.

Likewise, defining what is safe and getting everyone's input can be helpful (e.g., ask before going outside, staying with mom or dad when in the community, etc.). It is also a nice opportunity for parents to reinforce with their children their commitment to keeping everyone safe.

Periodic or regular family meetings can help set rules and expectations. Children can be encouraged to contribute their ideas, which can increase buy-in, with the understanding that the parent always has the final say.

Any time you add new rules or structure, your child is likely to test. They need to know where the limits and boundaries really are, so be prepared for this, and be prepared to be consistent.

Expectations

If your child has difficulty in the community or struggles in new places, sit down with them before you leave the house and go over with them the expectations for the outing. Then, have them repeat the expectations back to you. For instance:

Parent: We are going to the park. I expect you to walk with me the whole way and get permission from me before going over to the playground.
Child: Nods
Parent: What do I expect?
Child: For me to walk with you and get permission before going on the playground.
Parent: That's right. You can walk beside me, on your own, or hold my hand while we walk over (if your child chronically has difficulty walking with you, you may choose not to give them this choice and tell them that they need to hold your hand the whole way there). If you can't stay beside me, you'll need to hold my hand. So what are your choices?
Child: To walk next to you or hold your hand.

Parent: That's right. When it is time to come back home, what do I expect? (This has been discussed before, so the child knows the expectation).

Child: That I will come when you say with no fussing.

Parent: That is right. When it is time to go, you need to come right away with no fussing. Now, would you like to hold my hand, or do you want to try walking next to me by yourself?

Present a United Front

If you are co-parenting your child, or if your child has another care provider, perhaps a relative, childcare provider, or nanny, it is important to be on the same page.

All children will play their parents or caregivers against one another if they are allowed to do so, in order to gain wanted things (e.g., candy, toy, television time) or avoid unwanted things (e.g., having to discuss misbehavior, doing homework or chores). For some children with attachment injuries, it may have been a survival strategy, making the behavior all the more persistent.

Make sure all caregivers know and support your rules. Make sure you and your co-parent are in agreement regarding house rules and boundaries. Check in with each other regularly. If your child tells you that the other parent OK'd something, check with the other parent. Never undermine each other in front of your child. Discuss any parenting differences out of hearing of your child.

These simple strategies can avoid much aggravation.

Reduce Environmental Temptations

If you know your child flies into rages and becomes destructive, often throwing things, or, alternately, breaking others' things, do not have that heavy paperweight or the sentimental vase from your Great Aunt Dorothy where it could easily get thrown or broken. If property destruction is an issue for your child, put away fragile and valuable items for a time until you can trust your child to be around such objects.

Or perhaps your child goes crazy for candy. Don't expect to be able to leave a bag of candy where they can get to it without your child going through the whole bag. This can lead to sneaking, lying, and hoarding behavior.

You may say that children should learn to respect such limits, but even healthy, securely attached children may sneak a candy or cookie now and then. For an attachment-injured child, you may be coming up against a history of deprivation related to survival instincts; a history of being able to do what they want when they want; impulse control problems; and/or oppositional behavior. No need to make your job more difficult. Simply remove access to temptations. There is plenty to work on with your child.

If your child is destructive or tends to get into your things, it can also help to create a safe space for yourself, say your bedroom or office, and put a lock on it so you can feel secure about its contents when you are not in the room.

Provide Supervision

If your child is likely to hurt pets, younger children, or other vulnerable beings, don't leave them alone together. Provide supervision when they are together, and if you can't provide supervision, then separate them.

Likewise, for the internet and electronic devices such as phones. Research parental controls for computers and other devices, and monitor your child's use to ensure they are being safe and are not exposed to inappropriate material.

Limit Choices and Things

Attachment-injured children are notorious for having meltdowns when they have too many choices. If you can, limit choices to two or three options. This goes for toys too. Having too many toys available just seems to create chaos for the child. If your child has a lot of toys, you may want to rotate them, putting out a smaller selection of toys at a time.

Sometimes parents and others want to make up for a child's early deprivation by providing an overabundance of things at birthdays or holidays. This is not a useful strategy for the attachment-injured child. An overemphasis on things is counter to developing a healthy relationship between parent and child. It encourages the attachment-injured child to try to fill their inner needs with material things. This may lead to a pattern of first overvaluing an object and then quickly losing interest because, of course, things can never really fill emotional/relational needs.

Attachment-injured children will usually do best with a small, contained celebration where the emphasis is on celebrating family and child.

Holiday and Family Functions

Attachment-injured children should always be included in major family and holiday functions when possible. Loss of these should never be used as a consequence as this can injure the attachment you are trying so hard to foster and lead to extreme acting out. I have seen this occur with children young to old. Not including your child in important functions, that are child appropriate, will only reinforce the idea that they are bad and that you don't like or care for them. While your child should be included, it doesn't mean that you need to let your child ruin an event through negative behavior.

If your child is likely to have difficulty managing their behavior, then you may need to set some structure around the event. Some ways of doing that:

- Clearly state expectations before the event
- Have your child sit next to you
- Hold your child's hand as needed

- Limit the amount of time your child has at the event
- Have someone available to leave the event with your child if needed

Any accommodations should be discussed beforehand and always be framed as an attempt to help your child have a good time, not as a consequence. The message should be that your child is wanted and that you will do what you can to help them be successful. If your child cannot manage, the message should be, "We'll try again next time."

If you feel your child will simply not be able to manage at an event, then try planning an alternate event that they can manage. For instance, a large birthday party for Great Uncle Max may be too much for your child, but scheduling a special time for you and your child to get together with Great Uncle Max and give gifts and eat cake and ice cream may be doable.

Ease Transitions

Many children have difficulty with transitions, that is, moving from one activity, such as television time, to another activity, such as getting ready for bed. Your child may be one of them. Transitions from a preferred activity to a less preferred activity can be particularly difficult. A few tried and true strategies:

- **Give a warning** - Some children will transition better when given a 5 and/or 10-minute warning, and even a 2-minute warning if needed.
- **Use a timer** - You can tell your child, "I'm going to set the timer for _____ minutes. When the timer goes off, it will be time to...." Then when the timer goes off, in an upbeat tone, "Oh, the timer went off! It's time to..." The use of a timer helps take away the power struggle as it is the timer that is telling them to transition.
- **Help your child out** - This may mean offering a helping hand, "Oh, it is time to clean up. I can give you a hand if you

would like," or offering an extended hand, "let's go up to bed together," or engagement, "let's see what your homework is for today."

- **Make a game of it** - "Let's see how fast you can get your shoes on so we can go to Nana's," or, "I bet I can pick these up faster than you!"

Exercise, Nutrition, and Sleep

You do not want to be working against biology. All children need good nutrition, regular sleep, and regular exercise to be their best. Your child is no exception. Review your family diet to see if it might be contributing to difficulties. If you need more information on nutrition, consult your pediatrician or a nutritionist, or access the many online resources available. A regular bedtime, healthy food, and regular exercise will benefit your child.

Exercise also has many mental health benefits, including regulating mood, increasing happy hormones, and reducing stress hormones. It can be used as a coping skill in and of itself. See if there are some physical activities/sports that your child enjoys. If your child cannot manage on a regular team or program at this point, perhaps you can put up a basketball hoop, or you can take your child to the park regularly to kick a ball around or play on the playground.

Behavioral Considerations

While, as previously discussed, purely behavioral interventions are not sufficient for the attachment-injured child, some behavioral principles are helpful. Going against these behavioral principles can be like swimming upstream and may sabotage your work with your child.

Attention as Gold - Where Attention Goes, Behavior Flows

Unless your attachment-injured child is 100% disengaged, the coin of the realm is attention and emotional intensity. Be aware of where your attention goes. If it is constantly focused on negative behavior, then that behavior is likely to increase. Classroom studies bear this out, with behavior difficulties significantly lower in classrooms with a high ratio of positive comments to corrective comments.

Calmly dealing with misbehavior helps reduce the payoff for the child of that behavior. A very emotional or dramatic response to negative behavior can be reinforcing of that behavior. You may wonder why your child would want you to be mad at them or yell at them. If you consider that your child may not know how to get positive attention and/or may not know how to accept positive attention, but may crave attention, nevertheless, then it makes some sense. Negative attention may be the only kind of attention they know how to accept.

Also, for the child who has felt powerless, there is probably nothing in their world that feels more powerful than getting an adult, particularly their parent, dysregulated. It can feel like the cha-ching of hitting the jackpot for some children. Keeping this in mind, think about how you are responding to both positive and negative behaviors. While hurtful behavior should never be ignored, some negative behaviors can be strategically ignored while positive behaviors are given more attention.

Of course, it is not as simple with attachment-injured children as providing more praise for positive behaviors and giving less attention to negative behaviors. Remember that the child is working from a dysfunctional template or worldview. They often do not do well with overt or excessive praise because it creates cognitive dissonance. That is, it is at odds with their own internal beliefs about themselves, which can lead to further acting out behavior. For example, you say something very positive about your child, like what a great kid they are, but inside they do not believe they are a great kid. This creates internal tension, and they may just have to prove to you what a bad kid they really are.

So, what to do? A good way to acknowledge positive behavior without triggering resistance within your child is to just 'notice' it or acknowledge it in an understated way, often being specific, as in the following examples:

"I noticed you played well with your brother today."
"I appreciate your help with the groceries."
"Thanks for being quiet so I could read this."
"Good job following directions."
"Good idea."
"Good thinking."
"Thanks!"
"Good for you!"

Overall, work towards shifting your attention and intensity from negative behaviors to positive behaviors. The general consensus, based on research in classrooms, is that the ideal ratio of positive to corrective comments is at least 5:1. That is, at least five positive comments to each corrective comment.

If your child will accept more lavish or elaborate praise, then, by all means, provide it! Over time, as your child's story changes, they will be able to more easily accept positive feedback.

Use Attachment-Based Rewards

Do not offer things and treats as rewards for good behavior. For attachment-injured children, it does not work. They end up over-valuing things, shifting their attachment to objects rather than people. It is also an opportunity to manipulate for things, behaving for a reward and then acting out afterward.

Do offer extra time together, perhaps doing something special, as a natural positive consequence of your child's cooperation. For instance, "If we get all our chores done by 2 pm, you and I can... (make cookies together, play a game together, go out in the back yard together, take a walk or hike together...)." Again, choice can be emphasized when your child earns a positive attachment-based reward, e.g., "How nice that we can make cookies together! I'm so glad we both chose to get our chores done!"

Attachment-based rewards are anything special or extra that involves you and your child interacting in a positive way. Some examples include baking together, getting your hair or nails done together, going to a movie or performance, building a model together, etc. Of course, you can do these things unconditionally as well, not based on behavior, but doing something special together can be a nice treat for a job well done! By using attachment-based rewards, attachment is implicitly valued.

Avoid Intermittent Rewards

As a therapist, I was required to take a class in behavioral psychology. In that class, I learned about intermittent rewards. Intermittent rewards are rewards that are provided occasionally and randomly after a certain behavior. So say, for instance, your child tantrums to get what they want. Let's say you do not want your child to tantrum to get what they want. If most of the time you do not give in when they tantrum, but sometimes you do, then you are intermittently rewarding them for the behavior of tantrumming.

The two other alternatives are always giving in when they tantrum, or never giving in when they tantrum.

If you never give in when they tantrum, they may eventually give up on that behavior. In behavioral terms, we say the behavior has been extinguished.

If you always give in when they tantrum, then change to never giving in, the behavior will likely eventually extinguish as well, but it will take a little longer than if you had never given in.

If you sometimes give in when your child tantrums, and sometimes don't, then change to never giving in, research shows that the behavior will take much longer to extinguish than in the other two conditions. This makes sense if you think about it because your child has learned that you are inconsistent and you will eventually give in. Perhaps they just need to try a little harder. It takes a while longer to learn that this is no longer true.

The principle of intermittent rewards works for adults as well. Casinos bet on the power of intermittent rewards in gambling. Not only that, the intermittent reward of a win can be addictive.

For children, giving in occasionally for something you said "no" to when they whine, beg, or tantrum strongly reinforces that whining, begging, or tantrumming behavior. This is why consistency is so important.

Sometimes you may say no to a request that, upon further thought, you could say yes to. If your child is mature and skilled enough to talk with you appropriately (no whining, begging or tantrumming), fine, it may be OK to change your decision if you wish. You may want to observe, however, if that results in your child trying to negotiate every decision in a way that isn't productive.

Once your child starts begging, whining, or tantrumming, however, you will want to stay firm and hold the line. If you don't, every single "no" is likely to become more difficult. Being consistent may not reduce behavior at the moment and, in fact, may even exacerbate it, but it will reduce behavior over time. Remember that you are in it for the long game and never want to give up long term goals for short term relief.

Think about the concept of intermittent rewards for any behavior you want to decrease. Are there ways in which you are providing intermittent rewards for the behavior? How can you change that?

Be aware that if you have been inconsistent (and who hasn't) and become consistent, you will likely see your child's behavior become worse before it gets better. Don't give up, and don't give in.

Shaping

Shaping behavior is a technique in which you work to shape or move behavior in the direction that you want. You do this by rewarding or acknowledging behavior that is closer to what you want than your child's usual behavior.

For instance, if your child usually requires 3 or more repeats to follow a direction, but you notice that they complied on the second request this time, give them a brief nod towards that improvement, e.g., "I noticed that you followed directions better this time. Good for you!" Even though it wasn't perfect, don't sabotage your positive reinforcement by saying, "but next time, do it the first time I ask."

Another example: Your child snuck a cookie. Usually, your child lies about such misdeeds. Today your child admits that they took the cookie. Before addressing the cookie issue, acknowledge them for being honest, "Thanks for telling me! Good job. I appreciate that you told me the truth."

Stay alert to improved behavior. By acknowledging small improvements in behavior in the direction you want, you will help your child move closer to the desired behavior.

Communication

How you communicate with your child can have a direct impact on how cooperative your child is with you.

Eye Contact and Proximity

Before giving a direction or trying to have a discussion, make sure you have your child's attention using eye contact. If necessary, in an upbeat tone, say, "Look at me!" When they make eye contact, make sure your eye contact is soft and accepting, not angry.

Communicating with your child can be much more effective when you use proximity, that is, getting physically close to your child. Be close enough that you don't have to shout directions across a room, and get down to their level if possible.

Voice Tone

Voice tone can affect cooperation. Children will often respond to tone before content. When giving a direction, you want to avoid a pleading or begging tone of voice. When you use a pleading tone of voice, you have already given up your power, and you are not likely to get cooperation.

On the other hand, an angry, loud, and/or irritated voice tone may or may not get you what you want at the moment, but, either way, in the long term it is not likely to be effective. Your child may become triggered by your voice tone, increasing their reactivity, or, if used too often, they may simply learn to ignore it. Either way, they are likely to interpret a negative voice tone as confirming their badness and/or your meanness, getting in the way of the attachment you are working so hard to develop.

That does not mean you should walk on eggshells, however. Being tentative or afraid of saying the wrong thing is also not going to move you in the direction you want.

When giving a direction the first time or two, use an upbeat, clear, strong voice. After that, if needed, a serious but calm voice can be used.

Body Language

Just as your child may respond to your voice tone before your words, they may also respond more to your body language than your words.

If you are standing over them with your hands on your hips and a scowl on your face, it probably doesn't matter what words you use. Your child is likely to be reactive and defensive. They may even go into a fight or flight mode, depending on their earlier experiences, in which case they will not be able to hear what you have to say.

If possible, get down to your child's level and have an open, relaxed posture when you are trying to connect or communicate with your child.

Connect then Direct or Correct

Your child is playing quietly with their blocks. It is time to clean up, and you know your child is likely to have some difficulty. Perhaps you have given your child a warning, and maybe even used a timer, but your child still struggles. Try sitting next to them, putting a hand on their shoulder, and noticing what they have been doing. Pause a moment, then give a direction. It may look something like this:

> Oh, look what you built!... I see...you built a castle with green and blue blocs....(pause)...You did a nice job playing by yourself... The alarm went off, and you know what it means when the alarm goes off...Yep, now it is time to clean up...

If your child is doing something incorrectly, or something that they shouldn't, sometimes a simple connect and correct is all that is needed. Perhaps you see your child using something incorrectly. Walk over to them, get their attention and eye contact, say something positive or neutral, then give them the correction:

> Sweetie, look at me for a second (hand on shoulder if they will allow it). I see you are working hard on that. You've gotten a long way! That isn't how to use that tool. Let me show you.

Give Clear, Concise Directions

Keep your directions short. Do not string multiple directions together. Some children have difficulty processing or following through with long or complex directions, or it may just feel overwhelming to them. Use please and thank you as a matter of course.

Give Time to Respond

Give your child time to respond. Sometimes it may help to count silently to five or ten after giving a direction before repeating it or otherwise prompting. Some children just need a moment.

Direct, Don't Ask

Direct, do not ask your child when you want them to do, or not do, something. Asking your child sets you up for a "no" answer, which will ultimately make it harder for your child to comply. For instance:

"Please come set the table" vs. "Do you want to come set the table?"
"Time to clean up." vs. "Can you clean up?"
"Come sit next to me" vs. "Come sit next to me, OK?"

Use Positive Wording

Ask for what you want, not what you don't want. It takes longer for us to process a negative than a positive statement, and once we have processed that statement, we need to then decide what we are supposed to do. For instance, "Hands to yourself" is better than "Don't touch that," particularly if 'hands to yourself' is a phrase that is familiar to your child.

Come up with some short, concise phrases that address behavior concerns specific to your child. Some examples:

"Gentle hands!" vs. "Don't hit!"

"Talk respectfully!" vs. "Don't talk disrespectfully to me!" (a double negative here). If you use this often enough with your child, you may be able to even shorten it to, "Remember, respect!"

"Feet on the floor!" vs. "Get down from there!"

"Walking feet!" vs. "No running!"

Yes and Contingent Statements

Your child asks if they can watch TV. They have to do their homework first. You can respond in either of two ways:

"No, you have to do your homework first."

or

"Yes, you can watch TV after you finish your homework."

They both say the same thing, but the latter is going to be more palatable to your child. We all respond better when we hear a yes than when we hear a no.

Another example with dessert:

"No, you can't have dessert until you finish your dinner."

or

"Yes, you can have dessert just as soon as you finish your dinner."

Highlight Agreement and Commonality

There may be many things you and your child disagree on. It is natural to immediately respond to a statement we don't agree with by pointing out the disagreement. When having a discussion with your child, look first for the commonalities, what you can agree on, and state that before discussing the disagreement. This skill will help you in all your relationships! An example:

Child: Joey was mean today. He called me names and said no one likes me! I should have punched him in the mouth!"

While you might want to jump immediately to the idea that your child should not punch Joey in the mouth, it's more effective to say:

Parent: You are right. That was not a nice thing for Joey to say. It is not nice to call names or say mean things. Sounds like that made you mad (empathy statement). You did well, though, not punching him in the mouth.

At this point, you may want to talk through what might have happened if your child had punched Joey, or ask how your child was able to not punch Joey, what they did instead, framing that as the strong thing to do, and compliment on that choice or the strategies that allowed your child to make the better choice:

Parent: Oh, good thinking through it. Good job just walking away. I know it was hard, but when things are hard, and we do it anyway, that is being strong.

Give Reasons for your "No," within Reason

When you do have to say no to your child's request, it is not usually useful to just say, "because I said so." That gives your child the chance to imagine the worst, which is that you don't like or care about them. I know, you show them so many ways you do care about them, but remember, they are acting from a distorted worldview. In the absence of information, they will fall back on their negative expectations.

Keep your reason short and concise:

- Because it's almost dinner time.
- Because it is raining outside.
- Because we need to leave for school in a few minutes.
- Because it's not safe.

Don't let yourself get pulled into an argument about it. See the section later in this chapter on staying out of power struggles, and the section "Tips for Addressing Behavior Successfully" in chapter 11 for more about avoiding arguing.

You will almost always have a reason for your no's. If you find in some instance that you don't have a reason, consider if you have become in the habit of saying no, just as a matter of course. Or maybe the reason is just hard to articulate. For instance, maybe you are not sure your child can handle a new privilege. It is OK to say that, simply stating that you are not sure they are ready for that privilege yet, and let them know ways they can show you they are ready in the future.

If the "no" is just "not right now," then say so. If there is a time their request can be fulfilled, give them that information, but don't make promises you can't keep.

Give Choices, but Not Too Many

Attachment-injured children do not do well with too many choices, but a couple of choices, when appropriate, can give them a much-needed sense of control in their world.

Do you want to go to the park or play at home?
Do you want the green one or the red one?
Should we make cookies or muffins?
Should we watch this movie or that movie?

Also, when giving directions, it can help increase compliance by giving your child two acceptable choices, such as:

Do you want to hold my hand or walk by yourself?
Do you want to clean your room before lunch or after lunch?
You can pick these up by yourself, or I can help you. Which would you like?

Emphasize Choice

Emphasize choice. You want to help your child feel more empowered by understanding that what they do makes a difference. Your child always has choices, and each choice has subsequent consequences, i.e., "You can put your shoes on and come to ice cream with us, or you can stay home with Nana, your choice."

As another example, you may have a rule that if your child does not get ready for school on time, the next day, they will have to get up earlier to get ready for school. If your child is delaying getting ready for school, you can say something like, "Oh, it looks like you are choosing to get up earlier tomorrow so you'll have enough time to get ready."

Likewise, if your child is complaining about a consequence or result of behavior, you can say, "I'm sorry you made that choice," or, "You made that choice when you..."

Teach Skills

All children can use help learning to use their words effectively, identifying and expressing feelings, calming down, and problem solving. Children with attachment injuries may need more help than most. These skills can help your child better navigate the world and reduce behavioral difficulties.

Be patient in the teaching of these skills. Use repetition and, once taught, coach or prompt your child in real-life situations. This will help them to learn to use the skills spontaneously.

Help Your Child Find and Use Words

Some behavior may come from your child simply not having the words to express themselves; not being used to using words to get their needs met; and/or not feeling safe doing so. The short statement, "Use your words," in an upbeat tone, can become a staple in your communication with your child, particularly if they tend to react physically to frustration and other difficult emotions.

You can help your child find words by offering up suggestions:

Parent: (Noticing their child's physical signs of frustration). Are you having a hard time wrapping that present?"
Child: (nods)
Parent: Would you like help?
Child: (nods)
Parent: Can you say, "Help me please?"
Child: Help me please!
Parent: Good using your words!

Help your Child Identify and Express Feelings

Children often have difficulty identifying and expressing their feelings. This can lead to acting out. Any relevant parent/child therapy should be working on helping your child to communicate feelings, and to feel safe doing so with you. There are some things you can do to help.

You can help your child identify feelings spontaneously in the moment. For example, in the above example where the child is having difficulty wrapping a present, the parent can further add:

Parent: Looks like you're getting frustrated. Are you frustrated?

Additionally, there are games and activities I do with children and parents to help identify and express feelings that you can easily do at home. They involve the use of feeling cards. You can easily make some on index cards or purchase some (look for feelings flashcards). For the feelings matching game below, you need double cards. You want both feel-good emotions and more difficult emotions. The cards should include: Angry or Mad, Sad, Happy, Scared, Worried, Excited, Frustrated, and Calm or Peaceful. Search online for "feelings list" if you want more ideas for feeling words to use. You may just want to start with the above eight, and then expand as your child gets more capable and gains some mastery.

Here are some games to play with your child:

• **Feelings Charades** - This game can be played with any number of people. Have a list of feelings for reference for all to see, and cards with those same feelings on them. Have each person, in turn, pick a feeling card, and act out that feeling while the others try to guess the feeling. If only two or three people are playing, start with eight to ten feelings.

- **Feelings Matching Game** - Have pairs of feeling cards. Mix them up and place them face down. Like any memory game, take turns picking pairs and trying to find a match. If someone gets a match, they say a time when they felt that way, and they keep those cards. They can choose not to say a time they felt that way, but then they have to put the cards they picked back where they got them. Contrary to other memory games, if the person gets a match, they do not go again. The play passes on to the next person so that more people get turns. Sometimes a child may purposely not pick matches to avoid sharing feelings. In this case, use the Feeling Cards game, described below, the next time.

- **Feeling Cards** - Have a set of feeling cards. Spread the cards with just the backs showing and take turns picking a card. The parent picks the first feeling card and then tells the child a time they felt that way, starting with, "I felt _____ when..." Using the same emotion, the child then tells the parent a time they felt that way. Next turn, the child picks the card and shares, but, again, both parent and child tell about a time they felt that way. You might want to play the first time or two with only the easier emotions, i.e., happy, excited, calm, silly, etc., then add more challenging emotions in subsequent play. The play goes back and forth until all the cards are gone. If you want, and your child is ready, you can extend this activity to include reflective listening skills wherein each person reflects back what they heard the other say (see the section in chapter 6 on reflective listening).

- **Feeling Cards In-the-Moment** - Once your child is familiar with the feeling cards, they can be used in the moment to help them express themselves. For instance, if your child experienced a difficult event during the week, it may be helpful to pull out the feeling cards and go through them one by one, asking, "Did you feel (emotion) when that happened?" and separating out the cards that they acknowledge. At the end, you reflect back the feelings, "Oh, so you felt sad and mad and scared when..." You can further help your child explore their feelings by asking questions like, "What was scary about that for you?" or "What was the saddest part for you?" It can also be a good opportunity to talk about mixed feelings and how one often has several different, and possibly conflicting, feelings at the same time.

Teach & Practice Self-Calming Skills

You want your child to learn self-calming/self-soothing skills when they are calm and before they need it. This is something your therapist should be able to help you and your child with. Self-soothing or self-calming skills can include: deep breaths, counting to 10, counting backward, exercise, sensory activities such as running hands through sand, drawing, and positive self talk.

What works will vary with each child. Come up with some ideas with your child and pick two or three that you and your child can practice together when you are both calm, so it will be easier to access when upset. If you set up a calm cubby, you may want to put some materials for self-calming activities in or near the calm cubby.

Teach Problem Solving

Practicing problem solving skills helps children to slow down and think through situations. It also reinforces cause and effect thinking as possible solutions are evaluated for possible outcomes. If children can learn problem solving, it can also help reduce frustration and problematic behavior. This is something you may need to do with them for quite a while before they are ready, or able, to do it on their own. It is also a nice way to be there for your child. This is the POP CAR format for problem solving. There are others, but they all follow essentially the same simple steps:

1) **P**roblem - Identify the Problem
2) **O**ptions - Brainstorm Options
3) **P**ossible Outcomes - Consider Possible Outcomes of Ideas
4) **C**hoose
5) **A**ct
6) **R**eward - Reward Yourself

It would be good to sit down with your child and go over the steps and run through some examples. Then when your child is having a problem, it will be easier to address. In the process, don't do it all for your child. Let them generate ideas and help define the problem.

Suppose your child is being excluded by a couple of their peers:

Problem: being excluded
Options: approaching and talking it out with peers
yelling at peers (during brainstorming, write down
  all ideas without judgment).
playing with someone else
getting help from an adult
not going to school
helping the teacher during break time
Possible Outcomes: Go through the above ideas and discuss what might happen in each situation.
Choose: Will play with someone else.
Act: Act on the decision. Role-play ahead of time if helpful.
Reward: Check in with your child on their attempt and give a high-five, or other congratulatory response, for making the attempt (even if not very successful). Teach your child to pat themselves on the back for making the attempt, maybe saying something like, "good for me!"

Over time, your child may not only gain proficiency in problem solving, but they can further learn that they can be effective in the world and understand that their actions have consequences. Always, though, be available to help them.

Stay Out of Power Struggles

Attachment-injured children can be masters at engaging parents in power struggles. These are usually no-win situations for parents. By engaging, the parent may end up pushing their child to more extreme behaviors or may "win" at the expense of the relationship they are trying so hard to build. The following are some strategies to avoid a power struggle:

• **Broken Record** - Classic strategy in which you repeat a direction, calmly, until your child complies. Sometimes it is useful to reflect what your child says and/or provide some empathy, then continue to repeat the direction. If you can be consistent with this strategy, over time, you won't have to repeat yourself as much. Your child will learn that you mean what you say, and they can't draw you into an argument. An example:

The parent has already given the child a five-minute warning, and now it is time for the child to get ready to go.

Parent: It's time to finish up.
Child: That's not fair! I just started this!
Parent: Nevertheless, it's time to finish up, we have to go pick up your sister.
Child: Noooooo...I just started!
Parent: You just started, and that is frustrating, but still, it is time to go. You can work on that when we get back.
Child: YOU'RE MEAN! (Child is looking for a reaction here).
Parent: I hear you are frustrated, but it's still time to go.
Child: I'm not frustrated! You're just mean! (Still trying for the reaction)
Parent: Regardless, it is time to go.
Child: That's stupid!

Parent: Nevertheless, it is time to go.
Child: I don't want tooo...
Parent: I know you don't want to, but we need to go.
Child: Do I have to?
Parent: Yep, it is time to go.

• **Ignore the Hooks, Cover your Buttons** - Your child may try to draw you in with barbs or hooks. They may try to push your buttons. Any intense emotional response will feed their sense of power as well as their drive for negative attention and, therefore, will increase negative behavior.

• **Don't Argue** - Some children are masters of engaging their parents in arguments. I once knew a very bright four-year-old who was able to engage their parent in an argument about God. Clearly, this was not productive. Probably the most effective strategy to circumvent arguments is simply to say, "I'm not going to argue about this," and redirect the conversation or use the broken record strategy if necessary.

• **Take a Break** - If you find you are engaging in a power struggle, and particularly if your buttons have been pushed and you are being reactive, continued engagement will only fuel the power struggle. Sometimes it is important to give both your child and yourself space to calm down. If your buttons are pushed, it is even more important to disengage and give yourself time to calm.

If you have discussed "taking a break" ahead of time with your child, this may go more smoothly. In any case, you can state to your child, "I'm going to take a break so we can both calm down. I'll come back and talk with you in a few minutes."

During this time, really take a break. If you are still fuming and emotionally engaged, even while physically away, your child may pick up on this. Use your own self-soothing strategies. If there is something that engages you, like reading a novel or watching a brief clip on your phone, do this.

And, be sure to ALWAYS re-engage. If your child calms down and is playing quietly, it can be tempting to just let them be. It is important, though, as the parent, to re-engage your child. Otherwise, your child learns that they can push away closeness and engagement by arguing.

You do not need to necessarily go back to the power-struggle topic if it is not important. If your child tries to re-engage in the same power struggle, you can say, "Oh, I think we've talked enough about that. It's time to move on with our day," and then, move on with your day with your child. You can redirect to the next thing to be done or the next part of your day.

• **Let Go of Trying to Control Your Child** - This bears repeating. Your child needs to ultimately learn to control themselves. You can help them to gain control of themselves by implementing the strategies in this book, including building connection, structuring your home, and working with behaviors. The choices you make in any instance will increase or decrease behavior over time, but, in the moment, short of physical intervention, you can't control your child. By understanding this, unless it is a safety situation, you can give yourself a moment to consider your best response both for that moment and for the future, and avoid a power struggle.

Take Care of Yourself

Taking care of yourself is a preventative strategy. It is when you are tired, worn out, and feel you have nothing left to give, that you are most likely to under or overreact to your child, exacerbating behavior difficulties. You need to renew and refresh in order to be available for your child. Do not be a martyr to your child's behavior. It will only burn you out and make your child worse.

Find ways to take care of yourself. When you have a moment, get a massage, go for a walk in nature, have lunch with a friend, read your favorite author, dance like no one is watching, take a nap. Make a list of activities that are fun and/or nurturing for you. Put that list somewhere you can easily access. When we are tired and frazzled, it is usually much harder to come up with ideas to take care of ourselves. If you have your list close by, you can take a look when you have a few moments, and it will remind you of your options.

If you have a co-parent, trade off parenting when able or needed. Develop a support network. Find respite opportunities. If you are in a relationship with a spouse or other partner, make time for that relationship. If you have other children, make time for them as well.

These things are often easier said than done, but you can find ways to take care of yourself. Chapter 13: Self Care goes into further detail, providing some areas and questions to consider when exploring ways to take care of yourself.

Make a Plan

What are some new preventative strategies you would like to try? Be as specific as you can.

1._____

_____

2._____

_____

3._____

_____

4. _____

_____

5. _____

_____

11

Addressing Challenging Behavior

There are a few primary strategies you can use to address behavior with your child: Remind, Repeat, Redo, Rethink, Restore, and Givebacks. Note that none of these are likely to be successful if you are not working on building the connection with your child. Also note, if this is different from how you have been doing things, it will take time, and there may be some initial pushback from your child before you see consistent improvement in your child's behavior.

When your child is completely dysregulated, you will want to help them de-escalate before attempting any other strategies because, as previously stated, your child will be unable to process when they are in a fight, flight, or freeze mode. Trying to reason with them or consequence them in that moment will likely only further escalate the behavior.

If your child has done damage or been hurtful, however, you never want to let them off the hook entirely. At some point, when they are calm, maybe even the next day, work with them on restore and givebacks.

For unsafe behaviors, create a safety plan with your therapist or social worker.

Again, keep in mind that changing behavior will take time. If you are consistent with developing the relationship with your child, re-storying, implementing preventative strategies, and using these strategies for addressing behavior, it will likely get easier over time. Some of these strategies may take more time initially but will require less time in the long run, as your child becomes more cooperative. Be aware that the attachment injury may try to assert itself for a while through increased negative behavior before things get better. Be mentally prepared for that possibility.

Remind

Sometimes a simple reminder is all that is needed. If there are things you have been working on, it may be as simple as:

"Remember, respect!"
"Use your words!"
"Walking feet!"
"Who's in charge?"
"What was the agreement?"

Repeat

This strategy can help address non-compliance. It is the broken record technique and is mentioned in the last chapter under "Avoiding Power Struggles." The strategy is to simply repeat the direction calmly and firmly, using empathy statements as needed, until your child complies. Over time, the number of times you have to repeat yourself before your child complies should decrease if you are able to remain firm and persistent. An example is given in the last chapter, and here is another:

Suppose your child is supposed to do their chores before going out to play. You find, however, that your child has neglected to do their chore (unload the dishwasher) and is outside playing. You go outside, and in a positive, upbeat tone, you remind:

Parent: Tyrone, remember, chores before play!
Child: (ignores parent)
Parent: Tyrone, look at me! (positive voice tone)
Child: (looks up)
Parent: Chores first! You need to unload the dishwasher.
Child: Ah Mom, I'll do it later.
Parent: You need to do it now.
Child: Why? That's stupid!
Parent: Chores need to be done before we play. (Parent here ignores the "stupid" remark, as it likely would not have been productive, would have engaged the power struggle, and allowed the child to argue the point rather than complying). Alternately the parent could also have said, "You feel it is stupid, but, nevertheless, chores need to be done before play."
Child: But I just got started.
Parent: I understand you just got started, and that's frustrating (empathy statement). You can come back when you're done. Please come unload the dishwasher.
Child: I'll do it later!
Parent: Chores first. Come unload the dishwasher.
Child: (grumbles but comes towards the door)
Parent: Thank you. (parent here is acknowledging the wanted behavior (moving towards compliance) while ignoring the unwanted behavior (grumbling).
Child: I don't want to...

Parent: I know you don't want to. Thank you for doing something you don't want to do. It helps our whole family when everyone does their part.
Child: (reluctantly complies)
Parent: Thank you.

Note that the parent also could have used the 'Connect then Direct' strategy mentioned in the last chapter. To do this, the parent would have connected with the child first, perhaps coming over where the child was, making physical contact, commenting on the child's play, then reminding about chores.

Redo

Many behaviors can be corrected with a simple redo: You come into a building, your child starts running ahead. You say, "Walking Feet!" but they ignore you. You do not chase them, but when you catch up with them, you say, "Oops! Let's try that again with walking feet." You walk back to the beginning with them, then have them walk properly forward. Perhaps they take off again towards the end. You repeat. "Oops! Guess we have to try that again!" In this instance, you might want to give them the choice of holding your hand while they walk, or walking on their own. Once they have complied, a simple "Thank you" or "Good walking" will suffice.

Another example: You are walking by the cookie place in the mall. Your child demands of you, "Get me a cookie!"

You can say:

Parent: You want to try that again, respectfully?
Child: "Can I please have a cookie?"
Parent: Much better!

Now you don't have to necessarily say yes to the cookie just because your child asked respectfully. Your child needs to learn that demanding and whining will never get what they want, and speaking respectfully will increase their chances of getting what they want. If it makes sense to say yes, do so. If not, reply and give your reason:

"Good asking respectfully. It is almost dinner time, so we can't get a cookie right now (maybe you can buy a cookie to save for after dinner)"; or, "You've had enough sweets for today"; or, "We're having ice cream after dinner"; or whatever the reason.

As another example, perhaps the child in the previous scenario comes in to unload the dishwasher but does not complete the job. They leave dishes on the counter and silverware still in the dishwasher. If the parent knows their child is completely capable of emptying the dishwasher correctly, then they can simply keep redirecting them back, letting them know exactly what needs to be completed, until the job is done.

Redo's help your child practice appropriate behavior, which will strengthen the neural pathways for appropriate behavior. Once they have behaved correctly, move on. Unless, of course, they have done damage or injury. In which case, you want to consider restore and givebacks.

Rethink

If repeats and redo's aren't working, perhaps your child needs some think-time to reset. It may be useful to remove a child from a situation and have them take a moment. Think time is similar to a time in vs. a time out, in that you actually move your child closer to you, rather than away from you. It doesn't need to be a long think time. The intention is not to be punitive, but rather to stop whatever is happening and give your child a chance to refocus.

Perhaps you have repeatedly asked your child not to throw the ball in the house, but they continue to do so. You could say,

"Alicia, I need you to come sit over here and think about what you are doing for a minute." Perhaps you are working in the kitchen and can direct them to sit at the kitchen table. Give them a minute (use a timer if it is helpful), then:

Parent: (moves near child, gets down to child's level, and makes eye contact) Why do you think I asked you to take a minute?
Child: I don't know.
Parent: What did I tell you about the ball?
Child: That it was for outside.
Parent: That is right. So what are your choices?
Child: I can take the ball outside.
Parent: That is right. What are your other choices?
Child: I could play with something else?
Parent: That is right. You could take the ball outside, or you could play with something else. What do you want to do? (choices)

Continuing with the previous example of the child who is supposed to unload the dishwasher, if they continue to do the job incorrectly, you could have them take some think time for a minute to help them reset.

Restore

If your child does something destructive, like throwing things around, that can be cleaned up or restored, then that is the next level of intervention. If your child is emotionally dysregulated, which will be discussed later in this chapter, then wait until they are calm before having them do the restore. This may mean waiting until the next day if it is late in the evening, or until the afternoon if they have to get to school.

It may be tempting to clean up for them, as you can probably do it in a fraction of the time they can, but then the lesson is lost.

If they are young, or there is a lot to clean up, or they simply need the extra support, you can offer to help them. Similarly, if they broke something that can be fixed, have them fix it, with whatever support they need to get the job done.

By having your child restore any damage or mess, your child will learn that they are responsible for their actions, and they can make it right.

This is a good time to note that some behavior is self-rewarding. That is, the behavior itself feels rewarding. For instance, throwing and breaking things can feel good. More adults would probably do this (and some do) if there weren't societal costs associated with it. Having your child restore adds a cost to the behavior and will help them, over the long term, learn to better control themselves.

Givebacks

Sometimes your child may behave in a way that is hurtful to the family, parent, sibling, peer, or another person. Examples may be destroying property (e.g., breaking something that belongs to a parent or sibling), creating a disruption where the whole family has to change plans (e.g., acting out at a sibling's event wherein the whole family has to leave with the child, impacting a sibling's experience) or physical aggression.

In these circumstances, talk about givebacks. Givebacks are therapeutically important for your child. Your child will likely feel shame regarding the behavior, even if they appear shameless. Their own behavior has confirmed to them that they are bad, an underlying core belief. Givebacks allow your child to atone for their behavior and to be forgiven and forgive themselves, so they can move on and not continue to escalate.

Givebacks are a very important therapeutic process for both your child and your family. If your child has no consequence for hurting others, the behavior will likely continue, your child will get worse, and everyone in the family will feel like a victim of the attachment-injury driven behavior. Givebacks can be particularly important for siblings who may feel victimized.

When discussing givebacks, explain that when one person hurts or takes away from another, they have to give back to that person. Your child and the injured party, with your help, can brainstorm ideas for givebacks (e.g., doing sister's chores, sweeping the deck for Mom, repairing damages with dad, paying for repairs out of an allowance). It is explained, however, that it is not up to your child to decide what the giveback should be. Your child can give suggestions, but it is you, possibly with the injured party (e.g., a sibling), who gets to make the final decision on what the giveback should be.

Note that following through with your child on completing the giveback will often entail more work for you, the parent or caregiver, but follow-through is important, as the giveback is a therapeutic intervention for your child.

That being said, use givebacks selectively. Use them for the more serious offenses against others, particularly if your child frequently struggles with behavior. It won't be helpful if your child is overwhelmed by a backlog of givebacks, and the givebacks will lose their therapeutic effectiveness.

If you are using givebacks with your child, they should be used with other children in the home as well, as appropriate.

When Your Child is Emotionally Dysregulated

As noted, when your child is emotionally dysregulated, they won't be able to follow directions or think through situations. They need to calm first. Here are some ways of helping your child calm:

- **Self-Soothing Skills** - If you see your child becoming upset, you can try prompting self-calming/self-soothing skills that your child is familiar with and that you and your child have practiced together. This may include taking a deep breath, counting to 10, counting backward from 10, taking space in a special "quiet space" or "calm cubby," or other strategies. As discussed in chapter 10: Reducing Behavior, these skills should already be familiar to your child, having been practiced when calm.

  You can coach or prompt: "Take a breath. I'll take a breath with you," or, "Would you like to take a minute in your quiet space?"

  If they are receptive and willing to engage in this way, great! This is a great step in your child learning to control themselves.

  Often parents find that children with attachment injuries, when upset, do not want to cooperate. Even if they have mastered their self-calming skills, in a moment of anger, they do not want to cooperate with their parent. It is also possible that they are already too dysregulated to follow directions.

  Remember, with attachment injuries, your child may be particularly triggered by you due to your parent role and may be seeing you through an old, hurtful lens. If so, they are more likely to act out against you than to cooperate with you. If that is the case, sometimes empathy statements can shift the dynamic.

- **Empathy Statements** - Try using empathy statements while maintaining limits.

  Child: I DON'T WANT TO GO TO BED!!!!
  Parent: You don't want to go to bed!
  Child: YOU CAN'T MAKE ME! (starts throwing toys)
  Parent: You are really angry! You can be angry, but toys need to stay down.

Child: YOU HATE ME!
Parent: Oh, that is so hard, to think I hate you!
Child: YOU DO!!!
Parent: Oh, I can see how sad and hard that would be! I'm so sorry you feel unloved. (deep empathy)

If effective, the child may start to de-escalate at this point. Or, the child may need more empathy statements. If your child appears to be responding, you can then offer some nurturing:

Parent: Can I hold you while you are feeling so bad? Would that help?

If the child won't accept soothing, the parent can just stay near until the child is calm enough to move forward.

Parent: OK, I'll stay right here if you change your mind.

If the child starts playing with toys:

Parent: Oh! It's not playtime, it's time to get ready for bed. Can I help you?
Child: I don't want to go to bed! (at this point, the child is whining and not as dysregulated.)
Parent: I know you don't want to go to bed, but it is time for bed. You can play again tomorrow. Here, let me help you (parent offers a hand. If the child takes it, then yay!)

If the child shrinks away, parent moves back, offers a choice:

Parent: Do you want to go by yourself, or do you want my help?

Parent gives the child time to make a decision, repeats the question if needed.

This is a brief example. It may take longer and many more empathy statements to get to a place of cooperation.

Later, when your child is calm (in this instance the next day as the direction is for your child to go to bed) your child can restore, if needed, i.e., clean up any mess they made, and do a giveback if they have harmed anyone, or anyone's things.

Empathy statements are a good practice and often effective, but sometimes empathy statements don't work. In fact, I've seen children escalate further with empathy statements. In that instance, you may need to:

- **Give a little space and time** - If you notice that anything you say or do seems to make the situation worse, then the best thing you can do is to physically back up a little bit and wait. Stay within sight of your child. Take some breaths. Don't engage, but be present.

Sometimes your child's behavior will be feeding off of engagement with you, and no matter what you do or say, they escalate. If you have a parenting partner, it may be helpful to trade off at this point. Sometimes, switching out with a partner is all that is needed. But there may not be a parenting partner available, or switching out may make no difference. The child may continue to escalate with any attempt to intervene. In this instance, while staying physically present, you may need to emotionally disengage.

To disengage without triggering abandonment, you might say something like, "I can tell I'm not helping you. I'm going to stop talking, but when you are ready, I'm here." Then disengage - really disengage. Your child can sense your mental/emotional engagement. If you have a book you can read, a game on your phone, or some other way to mentally disengage, then do so.

If your child can tolerate your presence, you do want to stay within eyesight as a way to let them know that you are present for them, and are a resource for them, even if they don't know how to use you as a resource yet.

If your mere presence seems to be triggering for your child and they don't seem to be able to calm while you are present, you can move out of eyesight if needed, as long as you are not worried about their safety. Again, let them know that you will be back, "I'm going to go in the other room for a little bit. It looks like you need some space, but I'll come back in a few minutes."

Monitor your child and wait until they have calmed down to re-engage. And your child will calm down. Although it may seem to take forever, your child will eventually calm down. They always do.

At a later point, once they are calm, you can talk to them about what happened and do some problem solving, restores and givebacks if needed. Don't rush to do this. You want to give your child enough time to be in a calm space.

Some children will start to re-escalate when you try to talk to them about what has occurred. If that happens, tell them you can see they aren't ready to talk yet, they can take space if they need to, but they can't play until they are ready to talk. Let them know you'll continue to check back. Keep checking back. Don't allow them to escape this through tantrumming or the threat of a tantrum. If you can be very consistent, your child will eventually learn that this is what needs to happen.

If your child escalates to the point of safety concerns, you should have a safety plan developed by you and your therapist or social worker. Be proactive. If there is any likelihood of safety concerns for your child, develop a safety plan ahead of time.

Create a Safety Plan

If your child has unsafe behaviors, you want to be working closely with a therapist, social worker, or similar professional. Together you can create a safety plan. Unsafe behavior may include violence, self-harm, dangerous impulsive behavior like running into the street, runaway behavior, and sexually acting out behavior.

Have a safety plan ready before you need it. In a time of crisis, it is hard to think through options. A readily available plan will help you.

A safety plan is tailored to your child's specific needs. It should include what triggers unsafe behavior, how to de-escalate your child, and what to do if you are unable to help them de-escalate. It should include numbers to call for various levels of support, from friends or family to mental health crisis lines. The plan should clarify when to call outside resources, and all resources and contact information should be on your plan. The safety plan should be kept someplace readily accessible to you. You may want to make several copies to keep in different places and/or keep a copy on your phone.

Again, work with a professional on developing a plan. Any therapist or social worker working with you and your family should be able to help you do this.

The suggestions in this chapter are in no way meant to take the place of a safety plan.

Tips for Addressing Behavior Successfully

A Fresh Start

Once your child has corrected their behavior and/or completed their redo or restore or giveback, the episode is over. Everyone needs to be able to move on. A fresh start is needed to allow your child to move towards better behavior.

Separate your Child from their Behavior

Your child is going to make mistakes, and your child may even have extreme behavior. The message you want to give your child is that it is the behavior that is the problem, not your child. As discussed previously, if a child believes they are bad, then there is not much motivation to do well, so you want to avoid shaming and blaming statements like, "bad girl" or "bad boy!" Instead, you want to talk about the behavior, "It is not OK to hit Tommy. Let's talk about what happened and how to do something different."

Try to see your child's behavior as communication, a coping strategy, a sign of overwhelm, a way to express difficult feelings and/or a way to gain or avoid something, rather than as a defect in your child. Though it may be counterproductive at this time, their behavior may have helped them survive at an earlier time.

As discussed in givebacks, for hurtful behaviors, your child needs to make some kind of amends.

Externalize Behavior

You can take this a step further and work on externalizing behavior. This approach comes from a type of therapy called Narrative Therapy. In externalizing behavior, you further separate the behavior from your child and then can team with your child to overcome the behavior. For instance, if your child has difficulty with temper tantrums, which we will call "throwing a fit" for the purposes of this example, you can say something like:

Wow, that fit kind of got the better of you. You had to go to the principal's office and missed recess. Hmmm, I wonder how we could keep fits from causing you so much trouble...

Notice that it is the fit that is the problem, not the child. This opens up the space for problem solving.

Another example: Suppose your child is chronically defiant, saying "no" almost reflexively to any request. Due to defiant behavior, e.g., refusing to clean up and put their shoes on, they miss an opportunity to go sledding with their siblings and end up staying home. Your child is now sad at the missed opportunity. They say, "I wanted to go sledding!"

You sit next to them and put a hand on their shoulder. Now you could say, "Well, you should have gotten ready when I asked you!" This would be a natural response, and you wouldn't be wrong, but it is sure to evoke a defensive response from your child. Instead, you say:

> I wanted you to be able to go sledding too...Hmmm...It seems like defiance (or "a case of the no's") got in your way. It kept you from doing what you really wanted to do. I wonder how we could get defiance out of the way. It doesn't seem to be your friend...

Focus on how behavior causes problems for your child

Often parents and others try to tell a child how their behavior has caused problems for others (parents, family, peers). Until your child has developed a more secure attachment, however, they may not care. They may even be pleased to be causing others distress due to their anger and defense against their own pain; and/or the sense of power they gain from their effect upon others. So, initially, focus on how your child's behavior is causing problems for them, and try to move your child to a place of enlightened self-interest.

In the example in the last section, with the child who had a tantrum at school, the focus is on missing recess, not that the parent was inconvenienced by the call from the school.

As another example, if your child started screaming and yelling in the grocery store because you would not get them candy, such that you had to leave without checking out, rather than saying, "you ruined that outing for the whole family" (note, that this is also NOT separating the child from the behavior), you can say, "I'm sorry that fit got in the way of getting the groceries. Now we don't have your favorite cereal. Those fits sure are pesky!"

Employ Calm Persistence

Calm persistence will take you a long way in parenting. Your child will test and push for boundaries, particularly if you start doing things differently. Be the rock upon which the waves of your child's turmoil crash. Eventually, those waves will grow calmer. Your child will grow calmer when they know that you've got them; they can rely on you to be there and be consistent.

Don't Take Away the Things that Benefit Your Child

If your focus is on Restore and Givebacks, rather than being punitive or using general consequences, this probably won't happen, but it is worth saying anyway. If your child has something that seems to feed them as a person, where they experience success, you do not want to take that away from them as a consequence for behavior.

For instance, if your child is involved in sports, or a school club, or an art program that they enjoy and where they are doing well, taking that away from them for unrelated behavior will almost always be counterproductive. These kinds of activities can help your child grow emotionally and socially, and give them a productive place to channel their energies. While you don't want your child overwhelmed with activities, finding one thing your child really enjoys is a blessing.

Don't Chase Your Child - Stay Put

Children love to play chase! That's fine if you're playing tag in the backyard. Not so good when your child has been asked to set the table or is avoiding having that conversation about their behavior. It may be tempting to chase them, especially if your child is small and you can overtake them in two big steps, but your child will get bigger and will learn better chase strategies. Besides, that delight in their eyes as you go after them shows you how rewarding it is for them. Chasing a child is a no-win strategy for the parent.

The exception, of course, is in a truly dangerous situation, like a child running out onto a busy street. Unless it is for safety's sake, or truly play, you don't want to chase your child.

What you can do in those non-safety situations is to plant your feet, maybe even sit down to reinforce through body language that you are not going to chase them, then make a clear statement, calmly and firmly:

"I'm not going to chase you."

Followed by a direction:

"You need to come here."
"You need to set the table."

Or whatever is appropriate. If they still look like they are expecting you to chase them, repeat:

"I'm not going to chase you."

Use the broken record strategy if needed. Give them a little space to comply. If it is something that can wait, like discussing behavior, you can tell them:

"Take some time to think if you need to, and when you're ready, you need to come talk to me. No playing until you have talked to me."

Don't Argue with Your Child

Arguing is one of the ways your child is able to engage you while maintaining emotional distance. As such, it may be inherently rewarding for them. Some children are expert arguers, and arguing is always a no-win situation for the parent or caregiver. Arguing gives away your power to your child.

If you find you are arguing with your child, you can put a stop to it this way, using a calm, firm voice:

Parent: Oh, I'm not going to argue with you!
Child: blah blah blah blah blah....
Parent: I'm done. I'm not arguing (spoken calmly).

Remember, it does take two to argue. Once you have clearly stated your intention, you can try to redirect your child to do something else. If that doesn't work, you can walk away, or disengage, or simply stop talking, if your child persists. Of course, you want to make sure that at other times you are providing your child with adequate time and attention. Overall the goal is to help your child begin to accept appropriate, positive attention and move away from negative attention-seeking behavior.

Don't Over-Lecture

My general rule that I share with parents and caregivers is if you have explained something to your child three times, then you don't need to go into the explanation again (the exception may be if there are significant cognitive impairments). Just move on to the remind, repeat, redo, rethink, restore, or giveback as appropriate. Besides, if you talk at your child for a significant amount of time, they are just likely to tune you out.

If Your Child Lies

Lying can be challenging to address. If it is nonsense lying, like saying the sky is green, you can simply ignore it and redirect the conversation.

If it is an ego enhancing lie, like saying that they beat up a bully or scored all the goals in the soccer game, and you know for a fact it isn't true, you can either ignore and redirect, or respond with an empathy statement, like, "I bet sometimes you feel like beating up that bully! I can understand that, though it is important to control ourselves and not hurt others," or, "It sure would be fun to make all those goals!" If they insist that what they said is true, "I did beat him up!" or "I did score all the goals!" you can respond with, "Well, either way, I love you to the moon and back!" or "Well regardless, you are a star to me!"

If there seems to be an argument brewing, you can say, "Hey, I'm not going to argue about it," and again redirect and/or move on.

If your child is lying about misbehavior, and you know for a fact their part in the misbehavior, you have some choices. You can ignore the lie, saying, "I know you did....so now we need to talk about making it right."

Or you can have them take some think time, "Why don't you sit at the table for a few minutes and think about what happened and your part in it. When you are ready, we'll talk about it." If they do not change their story, then move on to the above statement about making it right. Do not engage in an argument about it. If they are able to reconsider and tell a truer story, give them kudos for that shift, "Thank you for being honest with me. I appreciate it."

In either case, follow through with redo or restore or givebacks as needed.

If you are not sure what happened and the offense is not serious, but you are pretty sure they are not telling the truth, then you can say something like, "Hmmm, I think something different happened, but I'm not going to argue about it. Some day I think you will trust me enough to tell the real story."

Putting it All Together

The following are a few examples of implementing some of the strategies in this book. The examples are probably somewhat shorter than what you might experience with your child, but they provide a sense of how the strategies can be applied.

EXAMPLE 1: The child, the toy, and the couch

In chapter 4, I described a situation where a child grabbed something from a sibling and ran behind the couch. Let's suppose the sibling has asked the child for the item back appropriately, but the child refuses.

The first thing to consider: Is this a safety situation? No, it is not. That means the parent has choices.

Parent: Michelle, you need to give that back to your brother.
Child: (just looks at you with a gleam in their eye, body tense, ready to sprint if you try to come after them)
Parent: I'm not going to chase you. You need to give the toy back. (refusing to chase, broken record)
Child: No! (looks at you, ready to spring into action if you come near)
Parent: (sits down) Oh, I'm not going to chase you. You need to give Joey back his toy. We can find another toy for you to play with.
Child: I don't want to.

Parent: I know you don't want to, but it is Joey's turn with that toy.
Child: (just stares)
Parent: Come here, let me help you.
Child: (looks away)
Parent: You can give Joey back the toy, or you can bring it to me. Your choice. (gives time to respond) (giving choices)
Child: Child crumples on the ground.
Parent: Do you want to hand the toy to Joey, or do you want to give it to me? (broken record, choices)

Hopefully, with persistence, the child will make a choice, and the situation will resolve. But this is also possible:

Child: I hate Joey! I hate you! (Breaks the toy and throws it.)
Parent: It looks like you are having some big feelings right now. (empathy statement) Take a breath. (self-calming skill) I want you to take a moment to think about what is happening. (gives child a moment) (think time)
Parent: How can I help you? You seem very upset, and I don't know why.
Child: You could give me candy. That would calm me down! (yes, I've seen children do this in a similar situation).
Parent: Sorry, that isn't an option. I could take deep breaths with you, though, or you could color for a few minutes or go to your calm space until you are ready to talk.
Child: (silence, still looking away)
Parent: Look at me!
Child: Looks at parent.
Parent: Thank you. Do you want to take some deep breaths with me or go to your calm cubby?
Child: I want to color!
Parent: Ok, sit down at the table. Here are your crayons and paper. I'll set the timer for ten minutes of calming time, then we will need to talk. (Note that the parent originally gave this as an option and so allowed it.)

Child: Comes to the table and starts coloring.

Parent stays in the vicinity of the child but busies themselves with other things. Parent may check in with the sibling, Joey, providing kudos for being patient and letting them handle the situation. After 10 minutes the parent sits down next to their child, who is coloring at the table, and puts their hand on child's shoulder. (connecting)

Parent: Look at what you are coloring. I see blue and green and red. (connecting)
Parent: Are you ready to talk?
Child: I want to go play!
Parent: You can go play after we talk. (contingent statement) Are you ready to talk, or do you need 10 more minutes of coloring? (choices)

If your child chooses 10 more minutes, you can reset the timer and say:

Parent: OK, you can have 10 more minutes, but then it will be time to talk. (Some children will want to keep extending indefinitely so you may need to set a limit like this.)

Note that sometimes children can talk more easily when their hands are busy. If your child is able to talk to you while they are coloring, it is OK to let them. If your child does better when they are not distracted:

Parent: You did a good job of calming down. Let's put this aside for a moment while we talk. (connect then direct)

At this point, the parent has some choices. They can approach their child with curiosity about what they were feeling and how they calmed, or they can use feeling cards as described in chapter 10 to help them identify feelings. If their child is willing to talk, then the parent can use reflective listening skills and empathy statements. One never knows what one will uncover. It may be their child had a problem at school or with a peer, and so had some feelings that they acted out at home. It also may be simply that they wanted that toy at that moment, and due to poor impulse control and difficulty delaying gratification, they took it. Or they may have no idea why they had this difficulty. That's OK. The parent can talk to them about what they could have done differently, using problem solving if useful, regardless. At some point, however, they need to get to givebacks:

Parent: I understand why you were upset. You broke something of Joey's, though. That took away from Joey. What do we need to do when we have taken away from someone else?
Child: A giveback?
Parent: That's right. Let's go talk with Joey and see what kind of giveback would be good.

It is important to note that there is another child in this scenario; in this case, a sibling, Joey. The parent doesn't want to totally ignore Joey. Some things the parent can do are let Joey know at the beginning that they will handle the situation at that point and, when their other child is taking think time, they can connect with Joey, thank him for his patience, and let him know they will be working with the other child to make it right. It is important that all the attention not always go to the child that is having behavioral difficulties. This can encourage other children to seek attention in negative ways.

When the parent goes with their child to discuss givebacks with Joey, they can also help Joey express how he feels, providing that feedback to the child that broke the toy, if it seems helpful. And, of course, Joey will benefit from the giveback.

EXAMPLE 2: I HATE YOU!

So you have set some kind of normal parenting limit with your child, perhaps telling them they can't watch that violent, gory show. Your child gets upset and screams at you, "I HATE YOU!" How do you respond? Well, you want to go for the underlying feeling:

Child: I HATE YOU!

Parent: You're really, really mad! (empathy)

Child: You ruin everything! I hate you!

Parent: How hard to feel like I ruin everything! That must feel so bad! (deep empathy)

Child: Joey and Suzy and Jalik get to watch it!

Parent: That is so hard when other kids get to. (empathy)

Child: You're mean! You hate me! Their parents are nice!

Parent: How hard that you feel like I hate you! That I'm trying to be mean to you! That must hurt a lot. I'm so sorry. (deep empathy).

Child: Then can I watch the show?

Parent: No, I'm sorry, each parent has to do what they think is best. I don't think that is a good show for kids. I love you so much, and I want to do what is best for you.

Child: That's stupid.

Parent: I'm sorry you feel that is stupid.

Child: Please, please, please. (whining)

Parent: No, I'm sorry.

Child: You're not sorry!

Parent: I'm sorry that this is hard for you.

Child: Ah, come on... (whining)

Parent: No

Child: Mommmm...

Parent: I'm not going to argue about it. (refusing to argue)

Child: (glowering)

Parent: Is there something else you would like to do or watch? (re-directing)

At this point, the child may allow themselves to be re-directed, or may try to continue to argue, or may stomp off and sulk. If they are re-directed, great. If they try to continue to argue, use the broken record strategy and refuse to argue. If they stomp off, give them space.

EXAMPLE 3: *The child and the figurine*

Imagine the following:

Your child has been playing quietly while you have been working in your home office. You find your child in their bedroom playing with toys. You sit down with your child, thank them for playing quietly, then comment on their play in an observational, non-judgmental way, "Oh I see you have been playing with the horses." (connecting)

At some point, you tell your child you are going to go into the kitchen and get a snack for the both of you. On the way to the kitchen, you notice that your bedroom door is open. You look in to see that a figurine that you value is broken on the ground. It appears to have been broken piece by piece. You had recently shown it to your child and talked about its value to you. You have a rule that your child is not allowed in your room without you. There is no one else in the house, and no other way this could have happened. You notice that you are becoming furious inside. What do you do?

First, acknowledge that you have a reason to be upset. You have a few minutes, so implement some self-soothing. Get support if you need to. In this case, you call your sister, making sure you are out of your child's hearing, and vent and get advice. She helps you calm. You go into the kitchen and prepare a snack, taking the time to think through your choices. Your impulse is to yell and scream at your child and come down hard on them. You've read the book; you know that that will just lock you into the picture they already have of you, confirm their "badness" and won't make things better in the long run. Still...

Your better nature wins out. You put the snack on the table and go to your child's room. You sit down next to your child again, "Snack is ready, but we have to talk first." Your child immediately knows what it is about and turns away from you.

"Do you know what we need to talk about?"

Child shakes their head.

"I went into my bedroom and saw that you broke my figurine."

"I DID NOT!"

"I know that you did. I wonder why you might have done that?" (curiosity)

"I DIDN'T! I don't know what you're talking about!"

"I think you do know."

"NO I DON'T"

"I'm going to give you a few minutes to think about it. I'll be right back." (refusing to argue, think time, taking a break)

You go back out to the kitchen, take a few deep breaths, remind yourself that you are in it for the long game.

You return to your child's room. They are curled up on the floor with their back to you. You sit down next to them and put a hand on their back. They don't pull away, so you leave your hand there. (connecting)

"OK, so I know you broke my figurine. Can you tell me what happened?

"I don't know."

"Hmmm..."

"It was an accident!"

"I'm not sure I believe that. You knew you were not supposed to go in my room, and you were not supposed to touch that."

Child is silent.

"I'm very curious about what was going on for you. Let's look at our feeling cards and see if we can figure out what you were feeling." You get the cards from the shelf. "Were you Mad?" (curiosity, identifying feelings)

Child shrugs

You go through all the feeling cards, and your child simply shrugs.

"Sounds like you don't know what you were feeling. I don't know what you were feeling either." You don't belabor the point. You move on to givebacks.

"So you have taken something away from me. You broke something that was important to me. What do we do when we take something away from someone?"

Child shrugs.

"We do a giveback, right?"

Child nods.

"Look at me!" (eye contact)

Child shakes their head.

"Look at me!" (positive, directive, upbeat voice)

Child glances at you.

"Good! Look at me again!" (shaping)

Child looks at you.

"I am sad that this happened, but I still love you. I need to think about what kind of giveback I need. You can think about it too while we have our snack. Are you ready for snack?"

Child nods.

"OK, let's go get snack, then we will talk about givebacks."

After snack, you brainstorm possible givebacks with your child. You remind your child that they can give ideas, but you get to ultimately decide. Note that if your child makes reasonable suggestions, you will likely get less resistance and more cooperation if you can choose an idea they suggest.

You decide that your child can weed the garden for you. You make a plan when this will happen and follow through.

After everything, you remind yourself that the damage to the figurine is done; no amount of screaming at your child would have brought it back. The fragile relationship with your child, however, has been strengthened. You decide to put a lock on your bedroom door until such time as you can trust your child. You pat yourself on your back for your good parenting choices and decide to treat yourself to your favorite lunch tomorrow while your child is at school. You call your sister back and let her know what happened and receive her support. Overall, it has been a good day.

Note that in the above example, the parent did a good job of staying out of power struggles. They did not engage in an argument about what was true, and when their child didn't respond to the feeling cards, they did not insist or force the issue.

The child, in this instance, did not respond to the feeling cards. That doesn't mean the parent should give up on this strategy. In a less stressful situation or when they were feeling less defensive, they may have had more success. Perhaps they had success with the cards in the past. Over time, the child will become more comfortable with the cards and more capable of identifying feelings.

The child also accepted physical touch (a hand on the back). Perhaps that was an improvement over previous incidents. If the child had moved away from the touch, the parent would have respected this, staying present and continuing the conversation.

In a similar scenario, the child might have become completely dysregulated when confronted, yelling, screaming, and throwing things. The parent would then want to support their child in calming, as described in chapter 11, before moving forward.

It is also possible that when it is time to give the giveback, the child will moan and complain. The parent would then just want to be consistent, using the repeat and redo strategies as needed. They can also point out that the child chose the giveback through their choices and actions (i.e., breaking the figurine) while declining to argue about it.

Yes, this is a lot of work. Over time, it should get easier, and the work put upfront will have rewards down the line.

Conclusion

Children with attachment injuries may, of course, respond differently than the children in these examples. It is hoped, however, that these examples can be useful to you in understanding how to implement strategies to reduce and address challenging behavior and assist you in your own work with your child.

Make a Plan

Identify a recurring behavior that your child struggles with, then lay out a plan of action to address it differently. Be as specific as you can.

Behavior: _____

_____

_____

Strategies:

1._____

_____

2._____

_____

3._____

_____

4. _____

_____

12

Getting Support

The phrase, "It takes a village," is never more true than with attachment-injured children. Don't feel you have to go it alone. Your child may need support on many levels, but you also need support. In this chapter, we will explore various types of support. Perhaps it will generate some new ideas for you.

Natural Supports

Natural supports are the people who are naturally in your life, generally family and friends. Family and friends can be invaluable in providing respite and emotional and moral support for you, and supervision and positive connections for your child.

It may be useful to make a list of all the family and friends you can think of and then, next to each name, write down the support each person can provide. You may be surprised to find that you have more available support than you realized. Don't be afraid to ask for help.

Perhaps your parent(s) would be happy to spend time with your child, but they aren't the best people to go to for advice (or maybe they are). Maybe your brother lives across the country but is great for a late-night phone call when you are at your wits' end. Perhaps you have a friend who has been through it with the school system and can provide valuable advice and support. Maybe you have family members who can be role models, or teach your child a new skill, or get involved in sports with them, or give your child a ride when needed. Think about your natural supports and what each can offer.

As best you can, make sure the people you choose to have in your child's life have some understanding of your child's dynamics and are supportive of you as a parent. You may have to educate them. It may help to provide information, such as this book or material from other reputable resources, to the people in your child's life.

Community Supports

Community supports are those supports that are readily available in your community. Are there community supports and programs that would be helpful to you and/or your child? Consider, perhaps, an after-school program or community recreation program, tutoring program or sports program, or a scouting or similar club-type program. Take care not to overbook your child. If they can handle it, try just one extra-curricular activity at a time. An activity that your child truly has an interest in, or at least is willing to give a try, can provide positive interactions and feedback for your child while giving you a little space and time as well.

Or, alternately, if your child can manage it and you are up for it, you might try parent/child programs where you can participate with your child in a sport or activity to further your connection.

Church and spiritual supports are worth exploring for both yourself and your child. Maybe a local church provides family-friendly or child-friendly services or events that would be helpful. Perhaps spiritual or pastoral counseling is available. Just be sure that the church's spiritual views and values are in line with your own.

Schools

Schools can be a major source of support or headache. Try to join with your child's school and work together. You may need to educate school members as to the needs and dynamics of children with attachment injuries. Most likely, all parties want the best for your child.

Schools have resources that may be useful to your child. They can assess your child for learning and emotional difficulties and develop an individual education plan if needed. This plan could include any number of services, including speech and language therapy, physical therapy, mental health support, or extra academic support.

Also, on an informal basis, an individual teacher may be a great resource for your child. One child I knew had difficulty on the playground, so the teacher was willing and able to have the child help them out in the classroom during breaks until the child was better able to manage socially.

You and your child have rights in the school system. If your child is having academic problems, be sure you know your rights. Usually, there is a right to an assessment and a determination if your child qualifies for extra services. You also have a right to contest any decision that is made. There are usually timelines in which a school needs to respond to a written request.

Do your research. Fortunately, with the internet, that is not too difficult. There are also for-hire school advocates and educational attorneys that can help you out. Or maybe your area has a non-profit agency that provides educational advocacy. Many school systems will have an educational advocate that you can access, but be aware that that person may steer you in the direction that the school prefers.

Professional Supports

Professional supports are those people who have specialized training and knowledge to help you and/or your child. As already mentioned, a therapist to work with you and your child is highly recommended and probably an absolute necessity. You should be able to turn to that person for any parenting concerns and issues related to your child.

But what about a therapist or counselor for yourself? Living with and working with attachment injuries can bring up a lot for a person. Perhaps you could use your own supportive therapy. Individual therapy could also help you explore your own family history or history of attachment, if that seems useful. Or perhaps you need a space to just focus on yourself and your other goals, separate from your child.

If you choose this support, just be sure that your personal therapist does not inadvertently undermine your work with your child by suggesting that it is hopeless or by being triggered themselves. I only mention this because I have seen it happen. In most instances, an individual therapist can be a great support.

If you are involved in a foster or adoption program, a social worker should be available to you, along with other supports. Do not be afraid to ask for help. Make full use of any support offered.

You can also call your local social service or mental health agencies, both public and private, and seek out help and resources. They may be able to offer, or refer you to, various levels of child and parent support.

Support Groups

Support groups allow you to know that you are not alone; you are not the only one going through this experience. They may also lead you to resources and provide helpful suggestions.

If you look online, you may find there are support groups for parents, adoptive parents, parents of challenging children, parents of children with attachment difficulties, single parents, parents with mental health difficulties, and more.

Some groups may be helpful, and some not. Avoid groups that are mostly negative. While it might be helpful to debrief your experience with your child, if there is no constructive or positive component to the group, it will likely be counterproductive.

Some places to look for groups include your local mental health clinics and agencies, social service agencies including adoptive and foster agencies, and even social media and online groups.

Respite

Respite is scheduled time for yourself, away from your child. Time and again, the support parents most often identify as useful is respite. Scour your family, friends, community, city, and state resources for respite opportunities that are safe for your child and will give you a much-needed break.

Media

This is the information age, and there is so much available if you take the time to look. You'll find books, blogs, articles, and websites. Be sure, though, to take a critical look at anything you find. The term Reactive Attachment Disorder, or RAD, has had a lot of very negative press. Therapies and parenting strategies for RAD have, at times, been harsh and/or overly controlling.

In Appendix B, I list a few well-respected authors in the field of child trauma and attachment.

Make a Plan

Are there some resources or areas of support you would like to explore further? Be as specific as you can.

1._____

_____

2._____

_____

3._____

_____

4. _____

_____

5. _____

_____

13

Self-Care

I gave self-care its own chapter because it is so important. While you do not have to be perfect to parent or care for your child, if you are constantly exhausted, burned out, and/or emotionally drained, you will not be the person your child needs, and you will not be happy with your parenting. You need to fill up your own well to be able to give to your child. Take a look at the following life areas and see where you can add a little care for yourself. Be careful not to pressure yourself. Be kind to yourself. This chapter is just a reminder.

For many, finding time is the most challenging part of self-care. You do deserve and need time for yourself. Avail yourself of all the resources, support persons, and services that can give you a little time and space for yourself.

As you read through the following areas (physical, mental, emotional, social, and spiritual) consider where you have needs and identify strategies and resources to help you meet those needs.

Physical

How are you taking care of yourself physically? Are you taking care of your basic needs for sleep and good food? How about exercise? Sometimes it can feel overwhelming to take an extra step, even for ourselves, but if it helps your overall functioning, it may give you back more energy than you put out. I have provided some ideas for thought and reflection. Consult professionals such as doctors, nutritionists, or personal trainers, if needed or helpful.

Food

Are you eating enough? Too much? Healthy food? Fast food and quick foods? Sugary foods?

Many people have a complicated relationship with food. Perhaps that is true for you. You may not feel you have time or energy to unravel all that, but maybe there are small changes you can make. If you do not feel you are eating as healthy as you would like, try finding one easy, small change for the better. When you feel successful with that, you can always add another.

Sleep

How are you doing here? Do you just need a good night's sleep? Can you make that happen? Do you have habits that interfere with sleep? Are there ways you can change that?

Exercise

Are you getting the exercise you need? Exercise is a natural stress reducer. It has so many physical and mental health benefits; it will pay you back in energy and well-being. There are so many ways to get exercise including walking, dancing, sports, gym and home workouts, and more. If you don't feel you are getting enough exercise, try to find something you enjoy and add it to your life.

Mental

We are intellectual beings. We were born with big brains and a natural curiosity. Take a look at your life. Do you have enough intellectual stimulation? Sometimes this might just mean making sure you have some adult time with others so you can relate on that level. Or maybe it means reading books of interest to you. Or perhaps taking a local recreation class of particular interest while someone provides care for your child. Perhaps your intellectual interest right now is on understanding your child and family dynamics, and reading this book is part of that. Maybe you like to do crossword puzzles or Sudoku. Whatever your interests, can you make some time for them?

Emotional

Give yourself a break. Be kind to yourself. Let yourself have feelings. Accept all your feelings.

Find time for yourself and do things that are soothing or fun for you, whether listening to your favorite music, being in nature, dancing, reading a novel, getting your hair done, hanging out with your pet, or whatever you find enjoyable and relaxing. Or just take a deep breath. A deep breath can sometimes be very helpful.

Therapy or supportive counseling for yourself can also be a way of taking care of yourself emotionally, as can debriefing with family or friends as needed. Likewise, some people find journaling a good way to process their experiences and emotions.

Mindfulness and gratitude practices have come to the fore as a way to get centered and to thrive. You might explore the many resources in mindfulness and gratitude to see if this is helpful for you.

You may already have some good emotional self-care strategies. If so, perhaps the first thing to do is identify what those strategies are. It may help to make a list of fun and/or soothing activities for yourself and keep it somewhere handy. When we are stressed, it can be much harder to think of ideas.

Social

We are also social beings. Make time for your relationships with all your children, your partner, extended family, and friends. This might mean a simple phone call now and then, lunch with a friend, a date night, or a special activity with each of your children. If you are feeling isolated, reach out. I bet you have friends you haven't talked to in a bit. Have a phone call or make a lunch date with one of them. Connect with people who you enjoy and who are positive. Avoid those who are negative and bring you down.

Spiritual

I have worked with parents and caregivers whose spiritual beliefs ranged from adamantly atheist to strongly religious. If you have spiritual beliefs that are important to you, do you have practices that help you connect spiritually? Practices could include meditation, or communing with nature, or praying, or attending religious services, or reading spiritual or inspirational books, or more.

Consider how your spiritual beliefs and practices can help you in your daily life, and if there are things you can do to develop that support and spiritual connection.

Make a Plan

In what ways would you like to take better care of yourself? Be as specific as you can.

1._____

_____

2._____

_____

3._____

_____

4. _____

_____

5. _____

_____

14

Attachment and Mental Health Diagnoses and Terms

Understanding diagnoses and terms associated with early trauma and attachment injuries can help you access and understand resources available to your child and interact effectively with support persons and professionals. This can be particularly useful when navigating the mental health system and conferring with therapists and other mental health professionals. This information is to help you be an informed participant in your child's care.

Demystifying Mental Health Diagnoses

Just about any psychotherapist or psychiatrist that gets reimbursed from a third party, whether it be private or public insurance, victim services, adoption funding, or any other source, is required to give the child a diagnosis in order to get paid. Therefore, if your child is, or has been, in therapy or received psychiatric services, they will likely have a mental health diagnosis that was determined by a therapist or psychiatrist.

So, where do these diagnoses come from, and how are they determined? The therapist or psychiatrist will conduct an assessment of your child, with your input, and likely a review of any records your child may have. Based on the assessment, they will determine a diagnosis.

The important thing to know about diagnoses is that they are a description of symptoms. If your child has the requisite number of symptoms for a diagnosis, they can be given that diagnosis. The symptoms can't be measured with a thermometer or a blood test. Some are observable behaviors, while others are internal feeling states. For the most part, there are no medical tests that can determine whether a child is depressed or anxious, has attention deficit hyperactivity disorder (ADHD), an attachment disorder, or any other mental health disorder.

Also important to note is that there is an overlap in symptoms between diagnoses. For instance, an anxious child may have the same short attention span and poor impulse control as a child with ADHD; or a depressed child may act out in ways similar to a child with oppositional defiant disorder. The diagnosis your child receives depends on how a practitioner interprets your child's symptoms. Children with multiple or complex symptoms may receive several diagnoses over time, and each new practitioner may interpret symptoms differently.

Children with moderate to severe attachment injuries tend to have multiple, complex, and confusing symptoms, so, over time, they tend to accumulate a variety of diagnoses. Very often, this does not include an attachment disorder diagnosis, as these are often reserved for children 5 and under, as will be discussed later, and/or practitioners may not be adept at recognizing or identifying attachment injuries.

The book, or bible, of mental health diagnoses is *The Diagnostic and Statistical Manual of Mental Disorders, Fifth*

Edition, known as DSM-5 for short. This is a 946-page reference manual published by the American Psychiatric Association that all western mental health practitioners are familiar with. This is where your child's mental health practitioner will be looking for, and confirming, diagnoses.

Some diagnoses related to attachment injuries will be discussed below. To see the exact criteria for any diagnosis, you can search "DSM-5 *(put diagnosis here)* criteria". Diagnoses are used to help direct treatment. If the primary area of injury for your child is relational, then a relationship-focused treatment is indicated.

Often attachment injuries underlie other diagnoses, and if the attachment injury is treated, symptoms will resolve. Sometimes a child has "co-occurring disorders," that is, they have more than one disorder occurring at the same time, in which case more than one diagnosis may be appropriate.

The DSM-5 has two attachment related diagnoses. The young child with significantly injured attachment will often respond in one of two ways with others, either with inhibited attachment or disinhibited attachment. In the DSM-5, these are accounted for in Reactive Attachment Disorder and Disinhibited Social Engagement Disorder, respectively. Note that in the prior edition, the DSM-4, these were identified as Reactive Attachment Disorder, inhibited type; and Reactive Attachment Disorder, disinhibited type. You may still see these references in the literature.

The DSM-5 descriptions of these diagnoses are rather narrow and do not capture the wide range of behaviors seen in children with severely injured attachment (such as nonsense lying or controlling behaviors). Furthermore, the DSM-5 diagnoses focus on children up to 5 years of age, and caution is suggested in making these diagnoses after age 5. Therefore, children 6 and over with attachment injuries are not well accounted for in these diagnoses. Unfortunately, the DSM-5 does not have a diagnosis that fits well for older children with attachment injuries.

There are several other mental health diagnoses commonly given to children with attachment injuries. Attachment-injured children may meet the DSM-5 criteria for Disruptive Mood Dysregulation Disorder, which is categorized as a depressive disorder. This disorder is new to DSM-5 and attempts to capture those children between ages 6 and 18 who have regular, severe temper tantrums, which are described as, "Severe recurrent temper outbursts manifested verbally (e.g., verbal rages) and/or behaviorally (e.g., physical aggression toward people or property) that are grossly out of proportion in intensity or duration to the situation or provocation." Additionally, mood is irritable and angry throughout the day. The DSM-5 criteria require that the temper outbursts and mood difficulties occur in at least 2 of 3 settings (home, school, peer). Some children with attachment injuries may fit these criteria, and some may not.

Eating, mood, and anxiety disorder diagnoses are also common, as are Oppositional Defiant Disorder and Conduct Disorder. Attention Deficit Hyperactivity Disorder (ADHD) is also sometimes attributed to these children.

Children with attachment injuries may or may not meet the criteria for posttraumatic stress disorder (PTSD). Like all DSM-5 diagnoses, to be diagnosed with PTSD, a person must generally meet certain specified criteria. The first of these is that the person has experienced trauma. Trauma is defined in the DSM-5 as "exposure to actual or threatened death, serious injury, or sexual violence" either directly to oneself; witnessing in person as event(s) occur to others; learning that traumatic events occurred to a family member; or repeated extreme exposure to the details of a traumatic event (as may occur with first responders).

Children with attachment injuries may or may not have experienced these kinds of events. Physical or emotional neglect or verbal abuse, which are not defined as trauma per the above definition, can lead to attachment injuries, as can early and repeated separations from primary caregivers.

Note that, whether or not they meet criteria for PTSD or for trauma as defined in the DSM-5, if a child has attachment injuries, the experiences that have lead to the attachment injuries are traumatic for the child in that they are scary and can be perceived by the young child as life-threatening. This results in deep anxiety and difficulty attaching.

There was a period when many attachment-injured children were being diagnosed with the somewhat controversial Pediatric Bipolar Disorder (not found in the DSM-5). Subsequent research indicates that these children more likely suffered from a depressive disorder, which is now better captured in Disruptive Mood Dysregulation Disorder.

As children with attachment injuries become older, if the underlying attachment injury is not addressed, some may be identified with "borderline" or "narcissistic" or "antisocial" traits; and untreated attachment injuries may develop into full-blown personality disorders as these children reach adulthood. Personality disorders are patterns of behavior and inner experiences that are dysfunctional, cause distress, and are very persistent and stable over time. Personality disorders are generally challenging to treat. Some examples of personality disorders that may be related to early attachment injuries include borderline, narcissistic, and antisocial personality disorders.

Child Trauma and Attachment Terms

To capture the type of early trauma and neglect experienced by young children that may result in attachment difficulties, a number of terms have surfaced in the literature. Below are some terms related to attachment and early trauma that you may encounter in talking to others or in other reading.

Adverse Childhood Experiences (ACE) Study

You may hear or have heard about the ACE study. This study was conducted by Kaiser Permanente and the Center for Disease Control. Over 1700 individuals were recruited between 1995 and 1997, with subsequent long-term follow-up for health and other outcomes. Subjects completed questionnaires about Adverse Childhood Experiences, including child physical, sexual and emotional abuse; physical and emotional neglect; exposure to domestic violence; household substance abuse and mental illness; parental separation or divorce; and household member incarceration.

The study found that adverse childhood experiences (ACEs) are common. Perhaps not surprisingly, the number of ACEs an individual experienced was associated with increased negative outcomes in physical health (injury, chronic illness, infectious disease, maternal health); mental health (depression, anxiety, suicide, and PTSD); substance abuse and risky behavior; and poorer education, career, and income outcomes.

This study was notable because it was the largest study of its kind with tracking over time. It confirmed what a lot of people perhaps already knew, i.e., that early difficult experiences can negatively affect many areas of one's life.

It is hoped that early intervention will help mitigate the impact of ACEs on an individual's life. That large scale study is yet to be done!

Attachment Injury

An attachment injury is an impairment or injury in a child's attachment to their primary caregiver.

Attachment Styles

In your reading, you may see references to attachment styles. Four primary attachment styles have been identified in the literature related to young children. An attachment style is the way a child connects to their parent or primary caregiver. There is secure attachment, which one wants to strive for, and then three patterns of insecure attachment: ambivalent, avoidant, and disorganized. All of the insecure patterns would indicate a child with an attachment injury. An insecure attachment style is the result of an attachment injury, just as a limp (a pattern of walking) can be the result of a leg injury.

These patterns were initially identified with toddlers, and so the definitions reference the behavior that occurs when these children are left in a "strange situation." The children were separated from their parent, exposed to a stranger, then reunited with their parent.

Ambivalent attachment (insecure): Child exhibits a very high level of distress when parent leaves. Upon parent's return, may approach, then avoid or push away. Also appears anxious around stranger adults.

Avoidant attachment (insecure): Child avoids caregiver and displays no preference between caregiver and complete stranger. This child does not seek out help or attention from adults.

Disorganized attachment (insecure): Child may exhibit a confused mix of behavior. May appear to freeze, be disoriented, wander, or have undirected or contradictory movement related to their caregiver.

Secure attachment: Child shows distress when separated from parent and happiness when reunited. Child will consistently seek comfort, security, and attention from parent.

This is a fascinating area of study, and recently there has been discussion and work related to adult attachment styles. All of this, however, is beyond the scope of this book.

Complex Trauma and Relational Trauma

Complex trauma occurs when someone has experienced multiple traumatic events. It is differentiated from single incident trauma in that single incident trauma is a one-off situation, while complex trauma results from multiple events over time.

The trauma is relational when it is interpersonal in nature. That is, relational trauma is the result of one person traumatizing another, as in the case of child abuse or severe neglect or domestic violence. This is as opposed to other types of trauma, such as a car accident or natural disaster.

Many children who have experienced complex or relational trauma have injured attachment, particularly if a caregiver was instrumental or complicit in the trauma. Not surprisingly, complex trauma is generally harder to treat than single incident trauma. The individual's sense of self and worldview are more greatly affected by complex relational trauma than single incident trauma.

Developmental Trauma

Developmental trauma is complex/relational trauma at a young age that disrupts normal development. Children with attachment injuries have experienced developmental trauma, as the attachment injury interferes with the child's normal, healthy emotional development.

Developmental Trauma Disorder

Developmental Trauma Disorder was proposed as a new diagnosis for inclusion in the DSM-5 in an attempt to capture and provide a framework for treatment for those children who had early and repeated exposure to trauma (including emotional abuse and separation from primary caregivers). Criteria included emotional and physiological dysregulation, attention and behavioral difficulties, difficulties with self-esteem/self-image, and relational difficulties, when these symptoms lasted at least 6 months and caused significant distress or impairment in functioning.

As discussed previously, children with attachment injuries are not well captured in existing diagnoses. Developmental Trauma Disorder was proposed in order to better identify these children, and may have been a better fit; this diagnosis, however, did not make it into the DSM-5.

Dyadic Therapy

Dyadic therapy is therapy that works with the parent-child pair or dyad. A dyad is simply a pair of individuals. A dyadic relationship is the relationship between those two individuals.

Many therapy models addressing attachment, including my own model, Multi-Modal Attachment Therapy (M-MAT), are largely dyadic, in that the healing of the child is presumed to occur primarily through the parent/child relationship. Once that relationship is addressed, a positive relationship template is created within the child, allowing them to function in other relationships.

Trauma-Informed

This term is used to denote approaches or programs that take trauma exposure into account. Trauma-informed care and trauma-informed practice are commonly used terms. Trauma-informed is a broad term that can be applied to many settings, including medical, academic, psychotherapy, and police services.

The idea is that when service providers have an understanding of trauma and the effects of trauma, they can respond in a more sensitive way to individuals with whom they interact. Agencies and organizations may develop specific "trauma-informed" practices to take trauma into account. This may be a teacher interacting with a student who has been exposed to domestic violence, a police officer interacting with a victim of sexual assault, or a medical provider working at a shelter for abused children.

If your child has been impacted by trauma, you may want to look for trauma-informed services, such as school settings. Trauma-informed is a current buzzword. If a service or program claims to be trauma-informed, don't hesitate to ask what that looks like and how they account for trauma in their practice.

Final Thoughts

No matter where you are in your relationship with your child, you and your child can move to a better place. All relationships have the capacity to grow and improve. Sometimes we need to walk through the deepest, darkest part of the forest, through the brambles and thickets, to get to the other side. Sometimes we need only look to the light and head in that direction. If you have even picked up this book, you are looking for that light, that direction. And you have the first, necessary ingredient to help your child; you care.

A friend recently reminded me that to get where you want to go, you need to start where you are. You need to be at the beginning before you can get to the end. Wherever you are with your child today, see it as the beginning, and each day a step towards your destination, a step towards growth in the relationship between you and your child.

If you are feeling overwhelmed by the information in this book, know that baby steps are fine. Start small. Pick one or two things to work on every day. Be proud of yourself for your effort and for caring. Celebrate small accomplishments.

To all reading these words, I hope this work has furthered you and your child on your journey together, and I wish you the best!

Appendix A

Attachment-Based Play Activities

Almost any playful activity that includes touch, eye contact, mirroring and/or rhythm will work for attachment-based play. Most games played with very young children will work. Avoid competitive and intellectual games. Be creative, but make sure the activity includes at least one of the critical elements: Touch, Eye Contact, Mirroring, Rhythm.

The relevant elements of each activity in this appendix are indicated by a letter following the description as so:

T: Touch; E: Eye Contact; M: Mirroring; R: Rhythm

The following activities have been collected from multiple sources. All attachment-based play must include Touch, Eye Contact, Mirroring and/or Rhythm. Any activities found online or through other sources should be evaluated for these elements. Other programs or sources may have different criteria for attachment-based play, and some activities may not meet these requirements.

Most of these games can be done with one or two parents, and some work well with more participants. Consider engaging the whole family in some attachment-based play!

Each game can be repeated several times in one sitting, and can be repeated over time. If your child has gained mastery in the game, some games, such as clapping games, can be altered to increase complexity or to go faster or slower, to add variety and challenge as needed. The games below are listed in alphabetical order.

All Around the Garden
Adult traces a circle on child's hand singing:
"All around the garden like a little mouse"
Then walks their fingers up the child's arm singing:
"One step, two step"
Then runs their fingers up the arm for a gentle tickle under the chin with:
"In your little house"
(T R)

Baby Powder Hand or Foot Prints
Lightly powder the child's hands or feet and make prints on black or dark paper. (T)

Blindfold Touch Walk
Child is blindfolded. One adult stands on one side with their hands on the child's wrist and arm, and another adult is on the other with a hand on the child's wrist and arm. Parents walk with the child around the room. Parents take turns having the child touch different objects and child guesses what they are touching. Have the child eventually touch the parent's hair or skin and guess. If appropriate (child is old enough/safe enough), parent and child can change places. This activity requires a level of trust and is usually better a little later in the development of your relationship with your child. (T)

Body Part Sounds
This one can be good for the reluctant child. The parent might discover that when they touch the child's foot it makes a "ring-a-ling" sound, and when they touch their nose it "beeps", etc. (T)

Body Part Touch
One person calls out a body part, such as "elbow" and then everyone touches elbows. This is good both for dyads and larger groups. (T)

Breathe Together
Parent and child hold hands. Parent leads and as they raise their hands, they breathe in, and as they lower their hands, they breathe out. Parent can coach "nice deep breaths". This is also good for teaching deep breathing. (T M R)

Clapping Games
Patty Cake, Double Double, or any other child clapping game will work. In these games you have non-threatening touch, rhythm and mirroring all at the same time! This can be done three ways with two parents and the child clapping together; or just between one parent and child. You can find any number of clapping games online. (T M R)

Clap Patterns
Parent starts by clapping a pattern. The child repeats the pattern in a call/response pattern. After parent takes a few turns, the child takes a turn to lead. (T M R)

Comparing Body Parts
A very simple game in which the parent and child compare the size or other aspects of body parts. For instance, putting hands up against each other's and seeing how big/small each is, or seeing how high child's head reaches on parents' body, etc. Can also compare color, shape, freckles, etc. Can also introduce

past and future orientation by saying things like, "I can remember when your hand was even smaller than this!" or "I bet you will grow up to be even taller than me someday!" (T M)

Eye Blink Pattern

Have the child look at the adult in the eye while the adult blinks a pattern (i.e., blink pause blink blink). The child then blinks the pattern back to the adult. The child can then have a turn to initiate the pattern. Very young children may find this too difficult. (E M)

Fast/Slow Clapping

The leader starts clapping at a steady pace, others clap with the leader. The leader then varies the pace of the clapping, faster and slower, while the others follow. Participants take turns being leader. (M R)

Feeling Faces

One person makes a face depicting an emotion, while looking at the other person. The other person copies that face and guesses the emotion. This can also be done in a group where the face is passed around the group. It is then the next person's turn. This is good, not only as a play activity, but also to help children identify emotions. (E M)

Follow-the-Leader

This can be done moving around the room in different ways, or it can be played while sitting down where you move your hands (i.e., clapping, patting your thighs, etc.) and possibly head in a rhythmic pattern. I usually make changes on counts of four, or multiples of four, making it easier to follow. The child can have a turn to be leader after the adults. (M R)

Gentle Touch

A very simple game to be used with children of all ages. I have at times used it every session as a closing to the play part of the session. Parent touches the child appropriately, gently, and child touches the parent back in the same way. It is then the child's turn to touch the parent in some appropriate way and the parent touches back in the same way. Repeat a number of times. (M R)

Hand Squeeze Message
Good for three or more people. All participants hold hands in a circle. The first person squeezes the hand of a person next to them in some kind of pattern such as "squeeze squeeze pause squeeze squeeze". That person passes the squeeze pattern on to the next person in the group and it goes around the circle back to the first person who says if it comes back the same as it went out. Even if it comes back completely different than it started, much positive feedback is given, "Yay! Good try! Let's try the other direction!" I often instruct participants to close their eyes, or at least not watch the squeezing as it goes around the circle. I also instruct them to keep the pattern simple, usually no more than 5 to 7 squeezes, depending on the age/ ability of the group. (T)

Hand Squeeze Pattern
Adult and child face each other holding hands. Adult starts and squeezes a pattern, i.e., left, left, right, right. Child squeezes back the same pattern. Participants can be instructed to maintain eye contact throughout, if desired. Then it is the child's turn. (T E M)

Hand Stack
Each person puts a hand in the stack and then their other hand, in the same order, so all the hands are stacked up. Then the person with their hand on the top moves it to the bottom, the next person does the same, etc. Start out slow. At some point you can reverse the order and the hand on the bottom moves to the top of the stack. Usually this game picks up speed until there is fun chaos. (T)

Itsy Bitsy Spider
Sing the classic song, but parent and child do movements together, i.e., each uses a hand and they work together to do the movement for the 'spider' moving up the water spout. This is tricky. Better for a little older child. (T R)

Looking for Colors in the Eyes
Parent tells child, "I want to see what colors are in your eyes today," and looks deeply in the child's eyes. "Today I see dark brown, but I see light brown too, like rootbeer color, and I would swear I see some gold!" Parent can ask what colors the child sees in their eyes. A nice game for non-threatening eye contact. (E)

Mirrors
Child and parent face each other. First the adult moves slowly and child follows, mirroring the adult, then the child leads. Parent and child can look into each other's eyes the whole time, and see if they can move together so that an observer cannot tell who is leading and who is following. This can be done either standing, using the whole body, or sitting just using hands and head movements. (E M)

Mother May I
This is best with two adults, one being the "caller" and the other advancing with the child. It is played the usual way, but directions include things like, "hug your child and take one step forward" or "move up to where your mother is and give her a high five". If child is sent back to start, I invariably give direction to parent, "go back to start, take your child's hand, and bring him X number of steps forward". Complexity of directions depend on age and ability of the child. I always have them reach me at the same time. Parent then gets a turn to direct. In this game, I never give the child a turn to direct, saying they are too young to be the "mother," thus maintaining the hierarchy. (T)

Motorboat, Motorboat

Participants stand in a circle holding hands. They move slowly in a circle singing, "motorboat, motorboat go so slow," they then pick up speed singing, "motorboat, motorboat go so fast," and finally, go even faster with "motorboat, motorboat step on the gas" until the parent calls "stop" and they freeze, then do the same thing in the opposite direction. (T R)

Peanut Butter – Jelly

One person says, "peanut butter," the others reply with "jelly" mimicking the same intonation/speed, etc. They do this a number of times changing tone, pitch, and speed (e.g., whispering slowly, or using a high, squeaky voice). (M)

Peek-A-Boo

Classic peek-a-boo. This is a good one to use when the child is shy and hiding their eyes. The adult can engage the child with a playful, "Where is _____. There they are!" as the adult discovers the child. They can then allow the child to hide again and repeat. If the child is strongly withdrawing, the adult can give the child additional blankets, etc., to hide behind, thus going with, rather than against, the resistance, and maybe at first only discovering a foot or elbow. (E)

Ring Around the Rosie (almost)

Hold hands in a circle and move clockwise or counterclockwise while singing the traditional "Ring around the Rosie" song, BUT at the end instead of "we all fall down," whoever is 'it' calls out a movement, such as "we all clap our hands" or "we all stamp our feet" and the participants engage in that movement, then it is the next person's turn. (T M R)

Rock-A-Bye-Baby (almost)

Parent holds or rocks child in whatever way is appropriate and comfortable while parent sings "Rock-a-bye-baby" song, BUT, replace the word "baby" with the child's name, and at the end, instead of "down will come baby, cradle and all" sing, "and I will catch *child's name* cradle and all." The parent can challenge the child to look at their eyes throughout the song, and repeat as appropriate. (T E R)

Row, Row, Row Your Boat (almost)
Child stands or sits between two adults. Adults hold hands making the 'boat'. Child puts their hands on the adults' hands. The adults row the boat to the song, moving forward and back. Have the child facing a parent and ask them if they can look into their parent's eyes the whole time, singing the song:

Row, row, row your boat gently down the stream,
Merrily, merrily, merrily, merrily *child's name* is such a dream!

Repeat as you want. As a variation, the eye contact can "power" the boat, with the adults rowing when eye contact is established, and stopping when eye contact is broken. (T E R)

Silly Faces
One person makes a silly face at the other person, then the other person copies it. They take turns. This one can also be done in a group, passing the silly face around the group. (E M)

Stand-Up – back to back
Two people sit down on the floor back to back with knees bent and feet on the floor. They interlock their arms, and try to stand up. This is better for older children and will not work if the size between the people is too different. (T)

Stand-Up – face to face
Two people sit down on the floor facing each other with feet touching toe to toe, and holding hands. They try to stand up together while continuing to hold hands. This is better for older children and will not work if the size between the people is too different. (T)

Staring Contest
Great for all ages! Two versions. First version, parent and child stare into each others' eyes, trying not to blink. Whoever can go without blinking the longest, wins. Second version, parent and child can blink, and can even make faces at each other. Whoever laughs first, loses. (E)

Thumb Wrestling
If you do not know how to play this, ask someone. Make sure it is all in fun and not too competitive. A good way to engage your child in non-threatening touch. Good for older children. (T)

Touch Guess
One person closes their eyes and the other person touches them as lightly as they can on their bare skin and they see if the person can feel it. Then they trade. (T)

Tracing Shapes or Letters on the Back
One person traces with their finger a shape or letter on the other person's back, and that person has to guess the shape. Then they switch. I usually start out with a piece of paper with six shapes drawn on it (e.g. square, circle, triangle, cross, star, zig-zag) and have the participants pick from that. When they demonstrate proficiency with this, they then use numbers or capital letters. (T)

Twinkle Twinkle (almost)
To the tune of Twinkle Twinkle Little Star adults sing to child:

Twinkle twinkle little star
What a special boy/girl/child you are
With (say some things about the child) e.g., long long hair
And a bright sweet smile
Strong strong legs
And a smart smart brain

Twinkle, twinkle little star
What a special boy/girl you are.

The adults in the room can use whatever special qualities about the child that they like. They can touch the child as appropriate on each body part that they are talking about and can trade off coming up with positive attributes of the child. (T R)

Appendix B

Resources

There is a lot of information out there. Here are some of my favorites!

Attachment-Based Parenting

These web pages were developed to share and support the ideas in this book.

www.m-mat.org/attachment-based-parenting
www.m-mat.org/resources

Attachment-Based Therapy

The following book, written by myself, describes a therapy model for working with children with attachment injuries and their families. The M-MAT model is consistent with the parenting ideas in this book.

M-MAT Multi-Modal Attachment Therapy: An Integrated Whole-Brain Approach to Attachment Injuries in Children and Families
by Catherine A. Young

website: *www.m-mat.org*

Communication

My favorite book on parent/child communication is the classic:

How to Talk so Kids Will Listen and Listen so Kids Will Talk
by Adele Faber and Elaine Mazlish

This book has been around awhile and there are now additional versions focused on very young children, and teens.

Picture Books

These wonderful picture books highlight the enduring parent/ child bond:

I'll Love You Forever
by Robert Munsch and Sheila McGraw

In My Heart
by Molly Bang

The Invisible String
by Patricia Karst and Joanne Lew-Vriethoff

I've Loved You Since Forever
by Hoda Kotb and Suzie Mason

No Matter What
by Debbie Gliori

The Runaway Bunny
by Margaret Wise Brown and Clement Hurd

Wherever You Are: My Love Will Find You
by Nancy Tillman

This delightful book highlights the specialness of your child:

On the Night You Were Born
by Nancy Tillman

Well-Respected Authors in the Field

The following are a few respected authors in the field of child trauma and attachment:

Bruce Perry, M.D., Ph.D
Daniel Siegel, M.D.
Bessel van der Kolk, M.D.

About the Author

Catherine Young, LMFT, is an author, trainer, consultant, clinical supervisor, child and family therapist and parent. She has devoted over 25 years to helping children and families in settings as varied as children's day treatment and intensive outpatient, adoption and foster family agencies, early childhood mental health, schools, juvenile probation, and private practice.

She is the creator of a new, practical therapy model for helping some of the most challenging children and their families: Multi-Modal Attachment Therapy (M-MAT). In her desire to share her ideas and bring healing to more children and families, she has authored two books:

On therapy:

M-MAT Multi-Modal Attachment Therapy: An Integrated Whole-Brain Approach to Attachment Injuries in Children and Families.

On parenting:

Understanding Attachment Injuries in Children and How to Help: A Guide for Parents and Caregivers.

CONTACT

Email: catherine@m-mat.org
Website: www.m-mat.org
M-MAT Training Institute: www.mmatti.org
Facebook:
www.facebook.com/MultiModalAttachmentTherapy
Youtube: M-MAT Training Institute ~ MMATTI
Instagram:
www.instagram.com/multi_modal_attachment_therapy